A NEW LIFE IN ISRAEL 1950-1954

A NEW LIFE IN ISRAEL 1950–1954

SHIMON REDLICH

Boston
2018

Library of Congress Cataloging-in-Publication Data

Names: Redlich, Shimon, 1935- author.

Title: A new life in Israel : 1950-1954 / Shimon Redlich.

Description: Boston, MA : Academic Studies Press, 2018. | Includes bibliographical references and index.

Identifiers: LCCN 2017043782 (print) | LCCN 2017044624 (ebook) | ISBN 9781618117175 (e-book) | ISBN 9781618117151 (hardback) | ISBN 9781618117168 (paperback)

Subjects: LCSH: Redlich, Shimon, 1935- | Jews, Ukrainian—Israel—Biography. | Holocaust survivors—Israel—Biography. | Israel—Biography. |

BISAC: BIOGRAPHY & AUTOBIOGRAPHY / Historical. | HISTORY / Middle East / Israel.

Classification: LCC DS113.8.U4 (ebook) | LCC DS113.8.U4 R43 2017 (print) | DDC 940.53/18092 [B]—dc23

LC record available at https://lccn.loc.gov/2017043782

©Academic Studies Press, 2018
ISBN 978-1-61811-715-1 (hardback)

ISBN 978-1-61811-716-8 (paperback)

ISBN 978-1-61811-717-5 (electronic)

Book design by Kryon Publishing Services (P) Ltd.
www.kryonpublishing.com

On the cover: *Grape Harvest*, by Ezra Tzamri.

Published by Academic Studies Press
28 Montfern Avenue
Brighton, MA 02135, USA
press@academicstudiespress.com
www.academicstudiespress.com

Table of Contents

Preface and Acknowledgments	vii
Chapter One	**01**
1 The Promised Land	01
Chapter Two	**16**
2 Kibbutz Merhavia	16
Chapter Three	**66**
3 Afula	66
Chapter Four	**96**
4 Training Base Four	96
Concluding Remarks	112
Bibliography	117
Index	120

For my *sabra* grandchildren Oria, Shai, Alon, Gal, and Shir

Preface and Acknowledgments

In this book, I tell the story of my new life in Israel in the early 1950s. My individual story is closely linked to the story of the newly established Jewish state and to the events that shaped its society in those years. After a childhood in Eastern Europe, I was a particle in an enormous wave of immigration that swept over Israel from all parts of the world, and I was among those who had to adapt to a completely new way of life. For close to two years, I lived in kibbutz Merhavia in Jezreel Valley. This *kibbutz*—a distinctively Israeli form of communal living—was the flagship community of one of the major pioneering movements, and it produced some of Israel's leading artists and statesmen. When I left the kibbutz, I moved to the nearby town of Afula and experienced small-town life in 1950s Israel. Subsequently, on graduating from high school in Afula, I was inducted into the army and went through "boot camp" at the famed "Training Base Four." In just those years—things would change afterward—the Israel Defense Forces (IDF) was a melting pot which had more foreign-born recruits serving in it than native Israelis. I was one of those who melted and melded in; in this book, I try to describe the transformation.

My "Israelization" occurred at its most intensive and rapid pace in kibbutz Merhavia. In those years, kibbutz life was regarded as the most "Israeli" and most desired mode of existence. Immigrant youngsters of my age who wanted to join a kibbutz usually did so as part of a peer group of immigrants from a similar locale; otherwise, they mostly joined their families in small towns or cities. I did neither of these. For better or worse, I was thrown right into the lion's den, with boys and girls who were mostly native-born Israelis—*sabras*—and whose parents were members of the kibbutz.

Later, when I moved from Merhavia and lived with my mother in Afula for the next few years, that was a regression of sorts; but, in some ways, life was more natural and easier for me in town than it had been on the kibbutz. The initial weeks of my army service as a recruit in Training Base Four weren't easy, but they left their mark and were crucial in the process of becoming Israeli.

This is the third and final book in a trilogy about my childhood and adolescence, with each book trying also to paint a picture of the historical contexts in which I grew up. The first book was about my childhood in prewar and wartime Brzezany, a town in eastern Galicia.[1] The second book dealt with my adolescence in postwar Lodz, in Poland.[2] As it has turned out, the research for the present book was more difficult and challenging than for the earlier ones. Being a professional historian with expertise in Eastern Europe assisted me greatly in the writing of those books. Yet the subject of Israel in the 1950s was completely new to me. I hope that I have caught and expressed the essence of Israel during that period. Regarding methodology, the reader will see that I draw heavily on vivid personal memories. Yet this book is not a memoir. I try to place the memories of my absorption into Israeli society within a wider historical context, using scholarly studies and archival sources. I also interviewed people who had lived in Merhavia and Afula in those years, as well as those I could find who had shared with me the trials of basic military training in the IDF.

Kibbutz life, as it existed upon my arrival in the country, has nearly disappeared. The image of the kibbutz and the popular national attitude toward it have altered considerably. Indeed, my personal perceptions of early 1950s Israel, and of the kibbutz in particular, have also changed— although perhaps not entirely in tandem with the national mood. Whereas for years after leaving Merhavia, I nourished ambivalent or even harsh feelings toward that place and its people, recent developments in Israeli society and in Israeli politics, in particular, have made me somewhat nostalgic for "those good old days."

The Israeli kibbutz has been extensively studied by historians and anthropologists. Studies of small Israeli towns are by comparison very scarce,

---

1 Shimon Redlich, *Together and Apart in Brzezany: Poles, Jews and Ukrainians, 1919–1945* (Bloomington, IN: Indiana University Press, 2002).
2 Shimon Redlich, *Life in Transit: Jews in Postwar Lodz, 1945–1950* (Boston: Academic Studies Press, 2010).

and so are studies concerning the IDF in those years—Training Base Four, in particular. For the latter, I was fortunate to also be able to draw on literary works, specifically the fine novel by Yehoshua Kenaz, *Infiltration*.[3] I've also greatly benefited from Oz Almog's socio-historical studies.[4] Last, but not least: I have made efforts in this book to look critically at my younger self, and to trace how I changed both physically and mentally as I grew into my new Israeli environment.

I'm immensely grateful to all my interviewees, with whose help I succeeded—at least partly—to relive my past. I wish to thank the staff of the Merhavia Archive for its prolonged and extensive assistance during my immersion into the history of the kibbutz. I am very grateful to the staff of the IDF Archive, who assisted me in locating source materials related to my basic military training. I'm not sure whether I could have conducted my research in Merhavia without the generous help of Yoel Mintzer and his wife, Ruthi. My meetings with the late Ezra Tsamri and his wife, Esther, enriched my understanding of their life stories. Ezra's artwork graces the cover of my book, and I thank Esther for letting me use it. More than once, I enjoyed the hospitality of my cousin Reuven Nir, one of the first children born in Merhavia. With him and with his younger brother, Yitzhak Nir, I discussed some of the intricacies of life in that kibbutz. I am also greatly indebted to Mrs. Mali Cohen and Ms. Natanela Bekler for their generous assistance. Mrs. Yocheved Granot sent me some excellent photos by her late husband David Granot (Dedi Grinshpon). Mr. Amos Ben-Arie shared with me his profound knowledge about Afula and his extensive research on his roots and family.

I would like to thank Professor Lazar Fleishman of Stanford University for recommending my manuscript to Academic Studies Press. I've discussed my Israeli project with Professors Oz Almog, Mordechai Altshuler, Omer Bartov, Yuval Lurie, Gabriel Finder and Terrence Evens, and with Dr. Avigdor Shachan.

Dr. Saadya Sternberg edited the initial manuscript of this book and I very much value his work and his advice. I am grateful also for the subsequent editing by Ms. Amanda C. Fisher.

---

3 Yehoshua Kenaz, *Infiltration* (South Royalton, VT: Zoland Books, 2003).
4 Oz Almog, *Farewell to 'Srulik': Changing Values among the Israeli Elite* [in Hebrew] (Haifa and Or Yehuda: Haifa University Publishers and Zmora-Bitan Publishers, 2004); Oz Almog, *The Sabra: The Creation of the New Jew* (Berkeley: University of California Press, 2000).

Thanks to Mr. Ofer Cohen of Tel Aviv's *Li Nof* Studio for his help with the pictures. I was very lucky to have the professional advice of Dr. Faith Wilson Stein and Dr. Oleh Kotsyuba of Academic Studies Press.

As always, I owe much to the patience and forbearance of my wife of the past fifty years, Judith Redlich, née Blumberg.

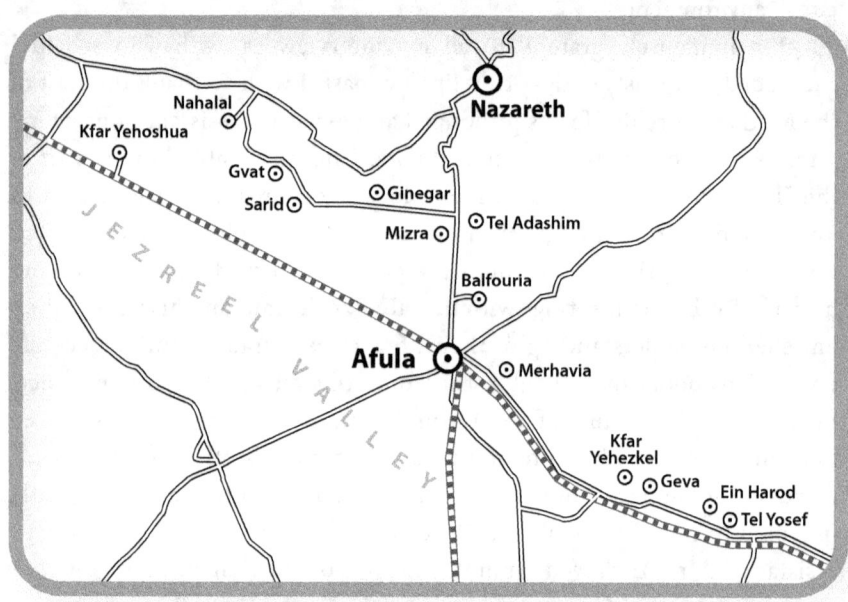

JEZREEL VALLEY

CHAPTER 1

The Promised Land

It was a sunny and cold morning: Tuesday, February 7, 1950. The *Galila* was approaching Israel's northern coast. A very unusual sight emerged as the ship neared Haifa. The Carmel mountain ridge came into view, all covered in snow. People began to gather on the upper deck. Someone began to intone the Hatikva; others joined in. Following a week-long voyage that had started near Venice we were finally getting to see the Promised Land. I was there with my mother. The previous afternoon, when the *Galila* had stopped a few miles outside the port, people called me and my mother onto deck. It turned out that my uncle Zeev—my mother's younger brother—was in a motorboat down below trying to locate us. Minutes later we were shouting back and forth at each other. These were the first moments of a reunion between two branches of a family separated by the war and the Holocaust. Zeev had reached Palestine as a young *chalutz*—pioneer—in the early 1920s. Pnina, a younger sister of my mother's, came a few years later and was among the founders of kibbutz Merhavia in Jezreel Valley. Zeev and his family lived in the nearby town of Afula. My father's sisters Rachel and Tsipora, who settled in Tel Aviv and Ramat Gan, arrived in Palestine in the 1930s. My mother, my aunt Malcia, and I were the only survivors of our large extended family.

My new life in Israel began that winter morning. Though I was aware for years that this had happened sometime in early 1950, I had no outside information about it. Only sixty years later and by complete chance did I come across details relating to that event and that sea journey. I had gone to London to participate in a showing of *Unzere Kinder*, a Yiddish-language film produced in Lodz after the war, in which I had performed as a child actor. Following the presentation, a man of about my age approached me and began speaking in English and Polish. It turned out that both of us had arrived in Israel at the same time and on the same ship. Within a day or two we were having tea in his London house, exchanging memories. Janek Geller, a business consultant fluent in several languages, showed me his personal documents, which helped me to retrace our itinerary from Poland to Israel. Our Israeli visas were issued at the Israeli legation in Warsaw in December 1949. Permission to pass through Austria and permission to stop along the way in Italy—this was granted in mid-January 1950. The train on which we traveled departed Warsaw on January 19, entered Austria on the twenty-first, and crossed the Italian border on the twenty-second.[1] The train journey must have been exciting, but I can barely recall it today. I do remember some of the stops. What amazed me when we passed the Italian border were the dark-skinned, black-haired men who were not Jewish. We were taken to a transit camp in Poveglia near Venice. The few buildings on the tiny island of Poveglia had previously served as a quarantine station and a hospital for the mentally ill. In local folklore it was always considered a spooky place. For me, Poveglia was mainly a transit site where we spent fewer than two weeks on our way to Israel. I recall a huge hall filled with bunk beds. It must have previously been a barracks. The food was quite poor: little dried-up rolls and spaghetti. It was there that, for the first time, I encountered oriental Jews. For years I would remember two pretty dark-skinned Jewish girls from Egypt who, like us, were on their way to Israel. Janek's parents arranged for a tour of Venice. We couldn't afford such luxury.

We boarded the *Galila* on February 2. The journey was to last a week. Certain images, sounds, and smells stand out in my mind. They were corroborated by Janek's memories. Part of the voyage, apparently near Crete, was stormy: many passengers became seasick. The strong smell of disinfectants was everywhere, especially in the crowded toilets. Those who could, preferred to stay up on the deck at all hours. I also recall, however, some pleasant moments when the dark-blue sea was quiet. Israeli music could be heard all over from the loudspeakers. I recognized some songs that I must have heard in Lodz. Among them were new Israeli hits performed by Shoshana Damari and Yaffa Yarkoni. Years later, I learned that the *Galila* had been built in the United States as a cruise ship before the First World War and had served for entertainment purposes along the Hudson River. During the Second World War it was requisitioned as a troop carrier. It was acquired by the shipping company ZIM in 1948 and for the next few years was used to bring Jewish immigrants, mostly Holocaust survivors, to Israel. After an interview with Nira Bleiberg-Hardof, a classmate of mine from Afula High School, she sent me some photos of the *Galila* dating from 1950 or 1951. Her husband Yoram, then a young cadet at

---

1 Janek Geller, interview by author, Tel Aviv, September 2011.

the Beyt Sefer Yami, a naval school in Haifa, was sent on a training trip to Venice on that same ship and brought back these photos. Small world![2]

Alona Frankel, who would become a popular children's author in Israel, had come over with her parents on the *Galila* a few weeks earlier. Her memories differed completely from mine. For Alona, twelve at the time, the *Galila* remained always *Galila mag'ila*—disgusting *Galila*. This was where she menstruated for the first time. Our differing memories may have stemmed from the fact that I was very much looking forward to my new life in Israel, following years of Zionist schooling in postwar Lodz. Alona's parents were communists and she didn't know a word of Hebrew. For her, the sea voyage and the change of worlds must have been traumatic. While I had a few mixed feelings, I was quite eager to face my new life.[3]

Another new immigrant who traveled on the *Galila* was the twenty-five year-old Ferenc Hoffman, who soon would have his name changed to Ephraim Kishon. He was a Holocaust survivor from Hungary who later would become Israel's leading humorist. Here is how he described his arrival: "The old slave ship *Galila* arrived at the port of Haifa with a cargo of new immigrants. Among them was yours truly, an emaciated and fearful young man. The Jewish Agency clerk asked him for his name and when he answered Ferenc, the clerk said: there is no such thing, and wrote 'Ephraim.' After that he Hebraicized his last name as well."[4]

The winter of 1950 was the harshest one in years. Headlines in *Haaretz* declared "Snow and Storms All Over the Country," adding the comment, "this is real winter, like in Eastern Europe." In kibbutz Merhavia, it snowed continuously for thirty hours, and the temperature dropped to minus eight degrees Celsius. In some places, the snow lasted a whole week. One kibbutz member recalled that "the slopes of Giv'at Hamoreh resembled Switzerland."

The weekly Merhavia bulletin spoke of a snow-clad kibbutz. The scenery changed completely. Trees broke and toppled. Tents were blown away. All transportation came to a halt. People were walking at night in snow-covered, moonlit fields enchanted by views that reminded them of their old country. Children and adults built snowmen and threw snowballs at each other. A little

---

2 Haifa City Museum website, accessed July 25, 2012, http://www.hms.org.il/Museum/Templates; Nira Hardof, e-mail to author, June 14, 2013.
3 Alona Frankel, *Teen Years* [in Hebrew] (Tel Aviv: Am Oved Publishers, 2009), 7–31.
4 Ephraim Kishon, *Partachia, My Love* [in Hebrew] (Tel Aviv: Sifriat Maariv Publishers, 1976), 8–10.

girl exclaimed, "from now on *khutz laaretz*—the lands abroad—will stay here and the kibbutz will be over there."[5]

At a get-together to celebrate my fiftieth birthday, I was showing family and friends old photos from postwar Lodz and from kibbutz Merhavia. In one photo from Lodz, dated December 1948, we are taking our leave of one of our teachers at the Hebrew school, who would soon be departing for Israel. The setting is quite official. Some of us are sitting in the front row. I'm the first on the right. The others behind us are standing. I'm wearing a dark jacket and a white shirt. My hair is neatly combed back and I look quite serene. In a picture taken in Merhavia, just two years later, the setting and mood are completely different. Three adolescents, two boys and a girl, are standing at the entrance to their communal quarters. I'm up front, bent forward so as not to block those behind me. The three of us wear identical casual gray jackets. My hair is a mess. Yet when I visited my family in Tel Aviv, I encountered very different styles of dress. My cousin David, a year older than me, used to go out in the evenings with his friends, in their upper teens. They were always neatly dressed in gabardine pants and impeccably white shirts, and they had shiny, sticky hairdos—just like James Dean. There was definitely a difference between the kibbutz and the city.

I recently opened a bundle of old, disintegrating letters. These were mailed from Brzezany to Palestine all through the 1920s and 1930s. Most were written by my mother and addressed to her sister Pnina in kibbutz Merhavia. Grandpa Fishl would add a few lines from time to time. The letters are in German or Polish, interspersed with some expressions in Hebrew. In spite of Pnina's new life in Palestine, family bonds were maintained. One postcard was from Soviet-ruled Brzezany, as late as 1940. Correspondence ceased in the wake of the German occupation, in the summer of 1941. It was only around 1946 that my mother wrote her first postwar letter to our relatives in Palestine. She complained that other Brzezany survivors had already managed to reestablish contact with their relatives in Palestine. "Why aren't we getting any letters?" she wondered. She went on to tell of our enormous loss: "Out of our extensive family in Brzezany and Kamionka only the four of us survived. I'm unable to tell you what we went through. I can hardly believe that I'm alive, having lost so many close and dear people. My only wish is to rejoin you as

---

5 *Haaretz*, February 6, 1950; *Bameshek, Information Bulletin of Kibbutz Merhavia*, February 10, 1950; David Cnaani, ed., *Sefer Merhavia, Kibbutz Hashomer Hatzair* [in Hebrew] (Merhavia: Sifriat Hapoalim Publishers, 1961), 138.

soon as possible." One of those letters to Palestine was a heartbreaking letter from my aunt Malcia. It spoke of her personal tragedy: "Imagine, I gave birth to two babies, a son and a daughter. One child died during the German times and the other just recently when I traveled to Lodz by train. It was only two weeks old." My mother kept repeating how hard she was working to get the necessary immigration papers. She also wrote about my longing to already be in *Eretz Israel*—the land of Israel. In one of the letters I added a few lines, in the Hebrew I had acquired recently at the Lodz Hebrew school. I asked my relatives' advice as to whether I should join *Aliyat Hanoar*—Youth Aliyah. I wanted to make sure that there would be a possibility to continue my schooling.[6]

My memories of the first days following disembarkation are scant and vague. I recall Aunt Pnina waiting for us at the Haifa port, among a small crowd of relatives and friends of the immigrants. She gave me a sandwich of bread and margarine. We were then taken to Sha'ar Ha'aliya transit camp near Haifa, but we didn't stay there long. Uncle Zeev brought us to Afula, to his nice and small newly built house, where I spent my first few weeks in the new country. Besides Zeev and Pepka, his second wife, there were three kids: my cousins Ora and Amos and a boy named Ofer.

What impressed me most was the neatness of the place and the prevailing bright colors of the rooms. How different from our dimly lit Lodz apartment on Gdanska Street! Ora showed me her collection of pictures of film actors and actresses. The radio played both familiar and new Israeli tunes, which I eagerly absorbed. Within a day or so I had my first haircut in the town center. The transition from huge and gray Lodz to small Afula seemed quite smooth and natural, perhaps because of our family. We soon met up with Pnina and her husband Shaya in nearby Merhavia. There was some talk about me starting school in Afula, but a few weeks later I was brought to the kibbutz, where I was to live for the next year and a half. The language of communication in Zeev's house was mainly Hebrew, with bits of Polish and Yiddish mixed in. Zeev's Polish was rather rusty; Pepka's, excellent.

I would get to know Afula later. In the meantime, the first meaningful and formative steps of my new life were taken in kibbutz Merhavia. It was there that I would actually turn into an Israeli. I was placed in the Merhavia boarding school in the early spring of 1950 and would remain there until the summer of 1951: less than a year and a half. However, the impact of these fifteen months was enormous.

---

6   Author's personal archive.

A New Life in Israel 1950–1954

❊ ❊ ❊

The immigrants who arrived at the port of Haifa on the *Galila* in early 1950 were just a tiny drop in an enormous wave of immigration that reached the shores of Israel during the first three years of the new state. Whereas on the eve of Israel's independence—in May 1948—the total Jewish population in the country numbered 650,000, by May 1951, that figure had reached 1.3 million. The newcomers originated in various European and non-European countries. Close to 110,000 people arrived from Eastern Europe in 1949, nearly half of them from Poland. The total number of immigrants in all of 1949 came to 240,000.[7] In 1950, another 170,000 immigrants arrived in Israel from various countries. The highest number in that year was in October, with close to 20,000 immigrants; the lowest, April, with slightly more than 8,000. Around 11,000 arrived in February 1950. We were among them.[8] Beginning in December 1949, trainloads of Jews left various points of departure in Poland in the direction of Italy. Each trainload carried five hundred to seven hundred passengers. The immigrants boarded Israeli ships either in Bari or Venice. We boarded the *Galila* in Venice. These immigrant ships were usually overcrowded. At times, the number of passengers was twice the ship's normal carrying capacity.[9] Shortly after disembarking, the immigrants were usually moved to a huge transit camp: Sha'ar Ha'aliya at St. Luke's, a former British army camp south of Haifa. Conditions there were harsh. People from different countries speaking various languages stood in lines to register and to receive food and bedding.[10]

Besides this huge camp, dozens of temporary immigrant camps were hastily set up throughout the country. More than 100,000 immigrants were sheltered in fifty-eight temporary camps in May of 1950. Within a year, a new type of immigrant dwelling compound—the *maabara* transit facility started replacing the initial camps. Close to 80,000 immigrants were still living in those first camps at the end of 1951, but another 180,000 were already living in the *maabarot*.[11] The maabarot were usually located near existing settlements.

---

7 Tom Segev, *1949—The First Israelis* [in Hebrew] (Jerusalem: Domino Publishers, 1984), 105.

8 Moshe Lissak, ed., *The History of the Jewish Community in Eretz-Israel since 1882: Israel—The First Decade* [in Hebrew] (Jerusalem: The Israel Academy for Sciences and Humanities and The Bialik Institute, 2009), 115–20.

9 Dvora Hacohen, *Immigrants in Turmoil: Mass Immigration and Its Absorption in Israel, 1948–1953* [in Hebrew] (Jerusalem: Ben Zvi Institute Publishers, 1994), 65.

10 Hacohen, *Immigrants in Turmoil*, 83.

11 Ibid., 326.

Some of the first ones were sited near Tiberias, Afula, Nahariya, and Hadera.[12] By late 1951, close to 260,000 immigrants were living in these maabarot and other temporary camps.[13] The largest maabarot, those housing between 5,000 and 8,000 residents each, were located in the center of the country, between Bat Yam in the South and Ra'anana in the North. Four smaller maabarot were set up near Afula, each housing fewer than 1,500 residents.[14]

European and non-European immigrants differed in the manner in which they were absorbed into the new country. Prior to Israel's independence, close to ninety percent of the *Yishuv*, the Jewish community in Palestine, was of European origin; and it was only natural that the absorbing society had more affinity for newcomers from Europe than for non-European immigrants.[15] But the patronizing attitude of veteran settlers was on the whole extended to newcomers, regardless of where they were from.[16] Some old-timers even considered their own newly-arrived relatives to be *golah*-type Jews: Jews of the diaspora.[17]

The kibbutzim absorbed only a small fraction of the immigrant population—most of them youngsters, members of the various Zionist youth movements. Eight thousand young people of Aliyat Hanoar settled in kibbutzim throughout Israel in 1948 and 1949.[18]

The kibbutz was a significant component of the Zionist settlement in Palestine and early Israel. The so-called "kibbutzniks"—the kibbutz settlers—symbolized the "New Jews" as opposed to the "Diaspora Jews." They were perceived not only as Zionist pioneers but also as the builders of a new, just, egalitarian, and morally perfect society.[19] The kibbutz movement's prestige and impact on Israeli society reached its peak in the early 1950s.[20] In the Yishuv and in

---

12 Ibid., 201.
13 Ibid., 298.
14 Ibid., 300.
15 Hanna Yablonka, "Immigrants from Europe and Holocaust Consciousness," in *The First Decade, 1948–1958* [in Hebrew], ed. Zvi Tsameret and Hanna Yablonka [in Hebrew] (Jerusalem: Ben Zvi Institute Publishers, 1997), 42.
16 Hacohen, *Immigrants in Turmoil*, 320.
17 Segev, *1949—The First Israelis*, 123.
18 Hacohen, *Immigrants in Turmoil*, 138.
19 Amos Elon, *The Israelis: Founders and Sons* (New York: Bantam Books, 1972), 172.
20 Elon, *The Israelis*, 410.

early Israeli society, kibbutz life was thought of as the elite form of socialist existence.[21] Around the 1950s, however, the kibbutz began to lose its centrality and special status. Its role in the absorption of the enormous immigration wave in that period was decidedly marginal. The great majority of post-independence immigrants lacked the ideological motivation to join the kibbutzim, and the kibbutzim had scant interest in absorbing great numbers of immigrants, lest they negatively affect the unique qualities of the kibbutz society. Israeli prime minister David Ben-Gurion had harsh words for "the pioneering movement's failure" to absorb the newcomers.[22]

The essence of kibbutz life was its communal nature. It was a collective meant to be based on openness, trust, and equality. It is possible these qualities truly existed in its early stages. In time, however, kibbutz society grew heterogeneous and variegated. The founding groups were people of like age who came from similar geographical, social, and cultural backgrounds. Over time, additional groups joined the initial settlers, and there were, of course, children born in the kibbutzim. Thus, one can speak of various cohorts within each kibbutz. While the subgroups did work to assimilate themselves into the collective, they also tended to band together.

The number of kibbutzim, as well as the overall kibbutz population, grew steadily in the 1930s and 1940s. Between 1935 and 1949 the number of kibbutzim increased from forty-five to 146. The overall kibbutz population grew from around 4,000 in 1932, to more than 47,000 in 1947, and over 49,000 in 1948. The kibbutz settlers comprised more than 7.6 percent of the Jewish population at that time.[23] Yet since the population of each kibbutz did not usually exceed a few hundred members, kibbutz society remained relatively small and intimate. One of the resulting features was the continuous closeness of day-to-day life in the kibbutz, which in turn resulted in a constant critique of the values of the other. Gossip was another characteristic; it functioned at least in part as a significant means for the society to exert its control.

While there were certainly some extremist and revolutionary ideas in respect to family life in the early stages of kibbutz society, the concept of

---

21 Henry Near, *The Kibbutz Movement: A History*, vol. 2, *Crisis and Achievement, 1939–1995* (Oxford: The Littman Library of Jewish Civilization, 2007), 1.
22 Anita Shapira, "The Kibbutz and the State," *The Jewish Review of Books* 2 (Summer 2010): 5–6.
23 Israel Shepher and Reuven Shapira, *Kibbutz: Continuity and Change* [in Hebrew] (Tel Aviv: The Open University of Israel, Unit 8–9, 1998), passim; Near, *The Kibbutz Movement*, 364.

a family and of parents with close bonds to their children still prevailed. All the same, children mostly lived away from their parents. From an early age, they led their lives mainly with their peers. The *metapelet*—nursery-school teacher—the teacher, and the youth-movement counselor replaced parents to a considerable extent.

The physical architecture of the kibbutz was affected by its concept and ideology as well as by practical conditions. Prior to permanent settlement, kibbutz group members usually lived in a tent encampment that could be easily relocated to meet shifting labor opportunities. Some tent camps continued to exist during the early phase of the permanent settlement, as well. Beginning in the 1920s and 1930s, signs of architectural planning could be discerned, with influences from the "Garden Suburb" concept and from early Soviet architecture. In time however, the Bauhaus style prevailed. Some of the most outstanding German-Jewish architects, who had immigrated to Palestine in the 1930s, were approached to plan various building projects in the kibbutzim. Preference was usually given to communal projects such as children's homes and dining halls. As for residential spaces, the tents were gradually replaced by wooden shacks, divided into several distinct units. The shacks in turn were replaced by permanent dwellings within which a single room was assigned to each couple. Communal showers and toilets were located nearby.[24]

The communal dining hall—the *khadar haokhel*—served as the social and cultural focal point of kibbutz life. Here, people met for meals, celebrated holidays, and convened for cultural events. Holidays and celebrations associated with nature and labor were most significant. There were theater-like performances, music, and singing. Often, furniture was moved aside to make space for dances. There was both collective dancing, the most prevalent form of it being the *hora*, and dancing in couples, in forms such as the *krakowiak*. In general, music held a significant place in the cultural life of the kibbutzim. The most popular instruments, taught to elementary-school children and high-school students, were the recorder and the mandolin.[25]

Assaf Inbari, in his book *Home*, tells the story of kibbutz Afikim, one of the largest kibbutzim in Israel. Afikim was founded in the hot and humid Jordan

---

24 Freddy Kahana, *Neither Town nor Village: The Architecture of the Kibbutz, 1910–1990* [in Hebrew] (Ramat Gan: Yad Tabenkin, 2011), passim.
25 Tamar Gispan-Grinberg, "Mural Art in the Communal Dining Halls of the Kibbutz Haartzi in the Years 1950–1967," *Cathedra* 135 (2010).

Valley in 1932 by a group of Hashomer Hatzair pioneers who had arrived in Palestine from Soviet Russia in the mid-1920s. They had come from such places as Moscow, Kiev, and Odessa. The most audacious of them dreamed of a large community of one hundred families. By the 1960s, there were close to 1,300 people living in Afikim.[26] Over time, the first founders from Russia were joined by settlers from Germany, Austria, and other European countries. "One could hear different languages in the communal dining room: Russian, German, Serbo-Croatian, Bulgarian, Hindu, Arabic, Yiddish, English."[27] Some of the later arrivals were Holocaust survivors. Inbari, with his distinctive, slightly cynical humor, implies that they didn't feel quite at home. Part of his story focuses on the 1950s, when the kibbutz had begun to change from a semi-utopian, egalitarian society to a more stratified and divergent community. German reparation payments to the Holocaust survivors caused quite a rift: "The Russian old timers, now in their fifties, told the camp survivors, now in their thirties, that if even one of them would accept an envelope with money without passing it on to the secretariat, the kibbutz as a way of life would cease to exist. The survivors, exhibiting their tattooed camp numbers, threatened to leave."[28]

Another point of friction was higher education. "A *teudat bagrut*—matriculation certificate—was superfluous and perhaps even dangerous to possess. A kibbutznik with such a certificate might even use it: he could leave the kibbutz!"[29] Inbari, a native son of Afikim, examines and relates the heroic and tragic story of "his" kibbutz, and of the kibbutzim in general, with his sense of humor and gentle irony.

Yael Neeman, in her book *We Were the Future*, tells the story of "her" kibbutz Yehiam in Western Galilee. Her narrative is a tapestry of personal memories and historical facts. The initial phase of the kibbutz's existence was linked with the 1948 War of Independence. The first group of close to a hundred settlers arrived there in the fall of 1946: "among them were young people from the Rehovot branch of Hashomer Hatzair, graduates of the Ben Shemen boarding school as well as people from Hungary and Slovakia, who had arrived just a few months earlier from postwar Europe." There was also another group of Hungarians who arrived in Yehiam after the War of Independence,

---

26 Assaf Inbari, *Home* [in Hebrew] (Tel Aviv: Yedioth Aharonoth Publishers, 2009), 184.
27 Inbari, *Home*, 201.
28 Ibid., 178.
29 Ibid., 206.

with somewhat different characteristics, but "the Israelis" and "the 1946 Hungarians" were always considered the founding fathers of the kibbutz. Over the years, additional groups joined kibbutz Yehiam, such as "the French" and the "South Americans."

The author extensively describes childhood in the kibbutz and her childhood in particular. What was most important to the adults, according to Neeman, was to build a community of children that would remain separate from their parents' world: "the intention—and hope—was to create a new child who would become a new man." And indeed, those children were the future. Stories were told and repeated about the first children of the kibbutz. More than once in the book she delves into the nature of the children's peer group, the *kvutza*: "we were born into the group called Narkis—Daffodil. There were sixteen of us: eight boys and eight girls. The group's name would accompany us for life." Toward the end of her book, Neeman touches upon the sensitive and the sad issue of leaving the kibbutz. She, herself, left Yehiam in 1981 when she was twenty-one. "A kibbutz is not just a village with a pastoral landscape. It's a political act. And we are deserters. Not traitors anymore, like we would have been ten years ago, but still we have to leave very quietly—on our tiptoes. We are no longer the sons and daughters of the kibbutz, but '*ozvim*,' quitters."[30]

The Spiros, an American anthropologist couple, made a study of childhood and adolescence in Beit Alfa—one of the first Hashomer Hatzair collective settlements in Palestine—during the early 1950s, when I was living in nearby Merhavia. Their research concerned the various stages of growing up in that kibbutz in those years. The basic and most intimate social unit for children in the kibbutz was the kvutza—the peer group. Each peer group was given a specific name, usually adopted from nature, history, or ideology. Children went through the nursery, the toddler's house, the kindergarten; completed primary schooling at age twelve; and had their secondary education at the boarding school—all as part of the same kvutza. Thus, a kibbutz child lived with his or her peer group from early childhood up until graduation from high school at age eighteen. Kibbutz members continued to be identified with the name of their peer group throughout their adult lives. Boys and girls slept in the same rooms, showered together, and often

---

30 Yael Neeman, *We Were the Future* [in Hebrew] (Tel Aviv: Achuzat Bayit Publishers, 2011), 15–16, 40–41, 72, 203.

ran around nude before getting dressed in the morning or after undressing in the evening.[31] Although from kindergarten and onward, group solidarity and identity were closely maintained, there was also verbal aggression, most of which consisted of name calling.[32] Living quarters and classrooms were usually located in the same building. Teaching was quite informal, as was the teacher-student relationship.[33]

The permanent core of each kvutza consisted of kibbutz-born boys and girls. In time, however, additional youngsters joined the peer group. These were the *yaldey khutz*—city children from broken or problematic families whose parents were ideologically close to the kibbutz movement. The day in boarding school started around seven in the morning. After classes and a short rest at noon, the youngsters would work for a few hours in the afternoon. Supper was usually followed by intensive social and cultural activities. What made kibbutz education different from formal education elsewhere was the "project method": instead of separate courses in history, geography, and literature, a specific historical period was examined, and various aspects of that period—such as economics, politics and science—were discussed.[34]

The Hashomer Hatzair youth movement was an integral part of life in the boarding school. Each peer group in the boarding school was also a kvutza within the movement, and all the peer groups constituted the local *ken* or nest. Each group had its *madrich*—counselor. The activities were quite similar to those of the Hashomer Hatzair youth movement in the cities: scouting, discussions, and ceremonies. Sports constituted a significant part of that life. Relationships within each kvutza were often complicated. Some youngsters were more popular than others. Some were rejected because of personal characteristics. Interpersonal aggression took the form of gossip, teasing, derision, and the use of derogatory nicknames. It was usually the yaldey khutz, the outsider children, mostly refugees and recent immigrants, who bore the brunt.

With regard to sex life among the teenagers, there seem to have been dichotomous views. Although sex was regarded by the kibbutz as a natural aspect of human life, sexual relations before graduation were strongly disapproved of.

---

31 Melford E. and Audrey G. Spiro, *Children of the Kibbutz* (Cambridge, MA: Harvard University Press, 1975), 221.
32 Spiro, *Children of the Kibbutz*, 154, 164.
33 Ibid., 262–63.
34 Ibid., 289–302.

The original peer group of kibbutz-born children in the boarding schools of the Kibbutz Haartzi movement shared rooms and showers, as that seemed quite natural to them. In time, however, especially following the arrival of the yaldey khutz, there was less willingness to continue this pattern. It was during the early 1950s that the communal showers began to be phased out. Heterosexual activity usually started around age fifteen and a few couples formed. Most of the contact took the form of necking; full intercourse was quite unusual, even among the senior groups.[35]

Another perspective on sex life in the kibbutzim I gained from Zeev Tzahor, or "Zevik" to his friends. He has been both my student and my colleague at Ben-Gurion University. We've spoken about kibbutz life on more than one occasion. Recently, I read his memoirs and was surprised to learn that he had joined kibbutz Ramat Hakovesh as a *yeled khutz*: at age fourteen, the same age I was when I arrived in Merhavia. However, whereas he was a *sabra*, or a "native," I was a Holocaust survivor. He started his kibbutz life in 1956; I arrived in Merhavia in 1950. There was, perhaps, another significant difference: Ramat Hakovesh was part of the rather moderate Ha Kibbutz Ha Meuchad movement, whereas Merhavia belonged to the radical leftist Hashomer Hatzair. What interested me most in his book were the quotes from the original diary of his adolescence in the kibbutz. I was surprised to find descriptions of his peers' erotic and sexual experiences. This is a topic that has always caught my attention.

Zevik observes from the start that the issue of boy-girl relations was significant for his peer group. In late December 1956, a few months after joining the group, he writes in his diary: "I don't have a girlfriend yet, however, the boys talk openly about the most personal affairs. My roommate tells me that at the first stage of necking boys and girls take off their shirts, girls take off their bras and there is a lot of kissing. At the next stage she massages his penis and he inserts his fingers while her panties are still on. The third stage is full sexual relations." What a difference from ascetic Merhavia! When I suggested to Zeev that the reason for this difference in sexual behavior stemmed from differing attitudes of the various kibbutz movements, he disagreed and argued that what made the difference was the wide variety of specific kibbutzim and not their ideological affiliations.[36]

---

35 Ibid., 328–34.
36 Zeev Tzahor, *We Were the Revival* [in Hebrew] (Tel Aviv: Hakibbutz Hameuchad Publishers, 2015), 55–56; Zeev Tzahor, personal communication, June 28, 2015.

Bruno Bettelheim, the renowned American psychoanalyst, studied kibbutz Ramat Yohanan in the early 1960s. He, too, paid special attention to the sociology of the peer group. His impression was that the in-group life made the kibbutz youngster inward oriented and suspicious of strangers. The adolescent, constantly surrounded by his peers, lacked a room of his own. Forming close friendships was difficult, especially between opposite sexes. Emotions were repressed and sexual desires needed to be sublimated. Another feature of adolescent life was the constant mutual- and self-examination. Bettelheim notes the overpowering emotions connected with leaving the group and the kibbutz, an act regarded as "desertion" and as "treason." Those who left harbored strong feelings of guilt.[37]

---

37   Bruno Bettelheim, *The Children of the Dream* (London: The Macmillan Company, 1969), 13, 211–24, 230–40, 269–71.

Figure 1.1 The immigrants' boat, the *Galila*.

CHAPTER 2

Kibbutz Merhavia

Ever since I started contemplating the possibility of writing about my time in Merhavia, I've been possessed with a desire to grasp the essence of this place and its people. While I was there, I had experienced Merhavia both physically and emotionally, but now I wanted to understand it. This time, as an adult with the benefit of hindsight; supplementing my own memories with those of others; and taking advantage of the tools I had gained over the years as a researcher and historian.

Merhavia was one of the first kibbutzim of Hashomer Hatzair in Palestine, and it was the political center of the Kibbutz Haartzi movement. For decades it was the home of its undisputed leader, Meir Yaari. And for years it was referred to, only half in jest, as the movement's "Kremlin." Perhaps ironically, this utterly secular flagship of the socialist kibbutzim had a name drawn from the Bible:

> From the confines, I called upon the Lord
> He answered me in the wide-open space [*merhav-ya*].
>   (Psalms 118:5)

There had already been a Jewish settlement at the site of the future kibbutz before the First World War. Indeed, Merhavia was the first Jewish settlement in Jezreel Valley. It was known at the time as the *kooperatzia*—the agricultural cooperative. Several groups of settlers arrived in and left the site over the two subsequent decades. Among them was a group of young Zionists from the United States. One of them, Golda Meirson from Milwaukee, would in time become Prime Minister Golda Meir.

The pioneers from Hashomer Hatzair arrived in Merhavia from Haifa in the fall of 1929. This was one of the three earliest Hashomer Hatzair communes to settle permanently in Palestine. The other two formed the kibbutzim of Beit Alfa and Mishmar Haemek. At that time, Merhavia was still being called "Herzliya," and it was one of the four Hashomer Hatzair kibbutzim that originally constituted the Kibbutz Haartzi movement. The pioneers who settled in Merhavia in 1929 had already been living and working communally in various locations in Palestine for four years before settling in the Valley. The group consisted of sixty-five adults and five children, the first sabras of the collective. The founding collective was augmented in time by several additional groups—*hashlamot*—assigned to Merhavia by the movement. Besides the hashlamot designated for permanent settlement in Merhavia itself, the kibbutz continuously hosted various training groups—referred to as *gar'inim*—that would eventually settle elsewhere. Ten such gar'inim got their training in Merhavia during the first two decades of its existence. From time to time Merhavia also hosted immigrant youth groups—*khevrot noar*. Up to 1960, Merhavia had hosted nine such groups. Merhavia also periodically absorbed single young men and women and a few elderly parents of kibbutz members. There was also a steady increase of kibbutz-born children, who in time became full-fledged members.

The first hashlama group, twenty-one members of Hashomer Hatzair from Poland, the Planty group, arrived in Merhavia in 1934. Yaari, during his mission to Poland in 1933, organized this hashlama for Merhavia, and demanded that the kibbutz accept them as full members upon their arrival. By 1940, the overall number of people in Merhavia—including members, children, parents, temporary residents, and youth groups—had reached 250. The number of full members of the kibbutz grew to 115. Another Hashomer Hatzair group, this time mostly from Tel Aviv, the *hashlama eretz-israelit*—consisting of over thirty young men and women, mostly sabras—joined Merhavia in 1941.

When the founding settlers arrived in Merhavia in 1929, they were in their mid-twenties. The Planty group members were in their early twenties when they came, and those of the Tel Aviv hashlama were younger still when they settled in the kibbutz. The Planty people were about ten years younger than the founders. The age difference between the founders and the 1941 hashlama members was close to twenty years. Two more hashlamot joined Merhavia during and immediately after the Second World War. The Neta group, which arrived in 1941, consisted of twenty-six members: ten from Slovakia and sixteen from Transylvania.

The number of full members of the kibbutz reached 150 in 1944, 175 in 1945, 200 in 1946, and 250 in 1950. These numbers include the native sons and daughters. The number of children and youth steadily increased. Whereas in 1944, 100 children of all ages lived in Merhavia, that figure grew to 130 in 1946, and to 200 in 1950. The birth of children has always been a significant event in the life of the community. When the kibbutz celebrated the birth of its one-hundredth child, Meir Yaari's daughter Rachel wrote a poem entitled *Megilat Hameah*—The Scroll of the Hundred—in which she listed the names of many of the sons and daughters of the kibbutz.[1]

As to the number of children per family, in the mid-1940s there were seventeen families with a single child, twenty-seven with two children, and just eight families with three children. The overall population of Merhavia in 1961 reached 650. Despite absorption and adjustment difficulties, only a small percentage of the founders and the various hashlamot left the kibbutz. Thus, out of the initial sixty-five founding members, only six left between 1930 and 1960. Of the Planty group, only four left, and a similar number dropped out of the 1941 hashlama.[2]

Who were the earliest settlers, the founders, who for years would shape the character of this specific kibbutz? Most had come from small towns in Polish eastern Galicia. Only a few were high-school graduates. The families they left behind in Poland after the First World War were mostly lower-middle class; Yiddish was their most spoken language. The young men and women of the Planty group who arrived in Merhavia in 1929 were of a higher educational level. They spoke Polish, Yiddish, and Hebrew. It should be noted that most of Hashomer Hatzair's publications were in Polish, and youth activities while in Poland were conducted in that language. Some kibbutz members continued to use their Polish-sounding first names, such as Janek, Kuba, or Ryszard. Although they were, in a sense, revolutionaries who had left the old country and dreamed of shaping the New Jewish Man in *Eretz Israel*, they brought with them to the new land an intimacy of the Jewish East European *shtetl*. Most corresponded with the families they'd left behind, and a few even went back for short visits.

A most significant social dilemma in Merhavia, as in many other kibbutzim, involved the absorption and integration of younger groups. The difficulties were, of course, faced mostly by the new arrivals themselves. The veterans and the newcomers, indeed, had much in common, such as the Socialist-Zionist ideology and the Hashomer Hatzair way of life. The Planty group who were all in their early twenties also shared a Polish-Jewish background and outlook with the founding members. At the same time, the newcomers had to face a

---

1 Bahevra newsletter, *Tishrey Tashach*, Merhavia Archive, Merhavia; Cnaani, *Sefer Merhavia*, passim.
2 Cnaani, *Sefer Merhavia*, 24–44; Bahevra newsletter, *Iyar Tashad*, Merhavia Archive; Aviva Halamish, *Meir Yaari—A Collective Biography: The First Fifty Years, 1897–1947* [in Hebrew] (Tel Aviv: Am Oved Publishers, 2013), 130.

completely new physical setting, whereas the older kibbutz members had already grown used to the new way of life. A leading member of the Planty group, David Handelsman, who changed his last name to Cnaani, recalls that they were brought from the Afula railroad station to Merhavia by horse and carriage. "Our first impression of Merhavia's central yard, the *khatser*, was one of repulsion. It was completely barren, lacking flowers or greenery of any kind. The khadar haokhel, the communal dining hall, with its wooden benches and cracked walls, was narrow and overcrowded. I almost pitied the residents. They were older than us and their women were prematurely wrinkled. A pang of anxiety struck at my heart: would this really become my home?" Although the difference in age was not all that great, according to Cnaani the Planty people were for years aware of a "glass wall" separating themselves from the founders.[3]

Apprehensions and doubts prevailed among the founding members as well. Some veteran members objected to any increase in the size of the kibbutz, others doubted whether the newcomers could be successfully integrated. A few months before the arrival of the Planty group, one of the old-timers wrote in the kibbutz newsletter, "Meir has succeeded in his mission; however this is only the beginning. Merhavia is about to be strengthened and invigorated by more than a quarter of its present membership. This is no slight matter. We must not approach them as twenty or so individuals but also as a collective." A major issue would be that of acculturation:

> These are people coming from a different country. They have been affected by a different culture and education. A certain manner of life has been formed over the years within our kibbutz, rooted indeed in the Hashomer Hatzair ideology, but with a unique Galician touch—Galician modesty, exaggerated earnestness, restrained romanticism and even some religious tunes. All those who joined us up till now faced a definite way of living and their only choice was to adjust to it. In the case of this *hashlama* group a whole new range of shades should be expected. It may not blend with the way of life we have consolidated.[4]

As for the "wide range of shades," the Planty group was indeed much less homogeneous than the founders' group. While still in Poland they received their training in a *hakhshara*—preparation program—which drew young people from all over Poland.

---

3 Cnaani, *Sefer Merhavia*, 250–52.
4 Y. Haleli, Bahevra newsletter, February 1934, Merhavia Archive.

The Palestinian group of 1941 differed completely from the Planty group. Whereas all the Planty members were Hashomer Hatzair people from Poland, the 1941 arrivals were movement people from Palestine, mainly from Tel Aviv. One of the most conspicuous members of the 1941 group was Avraham (Buma) Yassour. He stood out clearly at the group's meeting in December 1944, the event marking the completion of its first three years in Merhavia. Buma was a staunch Marxist, and often expressed himself via communist phraseology. At the center of the discussion was the problem of *aziva*—departure from the kibbutz—and its psycho-social implications. Buma, quoting his correspondence with Lusiek, another member of the hashlama who at the time was serving in the British Army, had very harsh words for those who decided to leave "under the guise of anti-Marxist arguments" and urged his colleagues "to not let emotions overwhelm reason." Buma maintained that "a social and ideological bond" was necessary to keep people together. He also remarked that the prevailing psycho-sexual depression among them was highly harmful. He disagreed with those who thought that there were simply not enough females and argued that "there is not sufficient intimate friendship and trust among us." Buma recommended such social activities as reading groups, ideological discussion groups and lectures, which would improve social cohesiveness. Shalom Lurie, another member of the 1941 group, was less critical of those who left: "It is hard for me to accept the fact that dear friends are leaving us. Some people apparently expected the kibbutz to be something which it isn't. There is indeed a gap between the dream and the reality." Another dilemma discussed at that meeting concerned the extent to which they should keep their group identity within the kibbutz while maintaining good relations with the founding members.[5]

The educational system in Merhavia consisted at first of a single kindergarten. When the first children reached school age in the early 1930s, they were sent to a school in Mishmar Haemek. Later on, the *khevrat yeladim*, the children's community, was founded in Merhavia; it combined an elementary school with communal living quarters for that age group. When the native children reached the age for secondary school, they were sent to Mishmar Haemek, which in those years ran the only communal boarding school for high-school students within the Kibbutz Haartzi. A local boarding school in Merhavia was launched only in 1946. The school year of 1946/1947 began with an enrollment of fifty-two children: twenty-five native kibbutz children; eleven yaldei

---

5   Bahevra newsletter, *Tevet Tashad*, Merhavia Archive.

khutz; and sixteen *yaldei gola*—Holocaust-survivor children. Everyday life in the boarding school was strictly planned and structured. The day began at six thirty in the morning. Classes began at seven forty-five and ended at twelve thirty. One to two in the afternoon was the daily rest hour, and two to four were the daily work hours, after which the youngsters took showers and had a small meal. Supper was served at seven. Social activities were held every evening of the week between seven thirty and nine.[6] The first group in the newly founded boarding school of Merhavia was named *Rimon*—pomegranate. It was later divided into two separate age-groups: an older one, *Shalhevet*—flame—and a younger one, *Khavatselet*—lily. The third age-group that joined them in the newly built boarding school was called *Gefen*—vine.

Since the number of native, kibbutz-born youngsters of high-school age wasn't sufficient to run a full-fledged boarding school, the kibbutz decided to also absorb yaldei khutz: mostly city children who couldn't live with their families for one reason or another. The Merhavia boarding school also took in a group of young Holocaust survivors from Czechoslovakia, the *Ayala*—gazelle—group. The number of youngsters of all categories who studied and lived in the local boarding school in 1960 came to 150.[7]

The most prominent member of kibbutz Merhavia was Meir Yaari. His life in Merhavia spanned more than half a century. He was not only a senior member of his own kibbutz but also the leader of the Kibbutz Haartzi movement in Palestine during both the British Mandate period and the first decades of the state. Yaari also would visit the centers of the Hashomer Hatzair in Europe, mainly in Poland. These formed the backbone of the worldwide movement prior to the Second World War.

Yaari was born as Meir Vald into a religious, Yiddish-speaking family in western Galicia, and arrived in Palestine in 1920. He was then in his early twenties. There, he met his future wife Anda, with whom he would later settle in Merhavia. Five years younger, Anda was born in eastern Galicia to non-observant Jewish parents; her native tongue was Polish. Their first child, Rachel, was born in 1923, six years before the kibbutz founders relocated to the

---

6 Shlomo Tallmon (Tillman), *The Way It Was: Merhavia*, 1931–1989 [in Hebrew] (Tel Aviv: Self-published, 1990), 48–51.
7 Cnaani, *Sefer Merhavia*, 306–13.

Valley. She was also the first child born to the founders' group. Their second child, Aviezer (Avik) was born in 1930. Yaari's relations with his family were affected by his work and life outside the kibbutz. Whereas early on, he was a loving father to Rachel, later, when his extra-familial obligations required much of his time and attention, relations with his second child Avik became less and less satisfactory, breaking into open conflict when Avik was a teenager living and studying at the communal boarding school in Mishmar Haemek. Their third child, Haim, was born in 1941, when Yaari was forty-four. Haim's suicide gravely affected the whole family.

Yaari was not an easy-going family man. He became increasingly grouchy with age, at times using his poor health to justify his harsh behavior. But he was close to his younger brother, Tuvia—also a member of the kibbutz. Tuvia took Anda to the nearby Eyn Harod health facility to give birth to Avik, and he often acted as a surrogate father when Meir was away. Tuvia adored his older brother. However, Meir's relations with his older brother, Moshe, the firstborn, were complex from early childhood and remained so throughout their lives.[8]

Yaari, who spent long periods of time outside the kibbutz—both in Tel Aviv and abroad—"was never an ordinary kibbutz member," according to his biographer Aviva Halamish.[9] His relations with the people in Merhavia were extremely complex. On the one hand, he was regarded as a father figure. On the other hand, he was criticized and envied for his special status. Yaari often spoke of his great love for his native kibbutz but at the same time must have envied Yaakov Hazan—another prominent movement leader, who, unlike Yaari, enjoyed warm personal relations with the members of his kibbutz, Mishmar Haemek.[10]

Yaari belonged to that small group of kibbutz leaders who were often active outside the close-knit kibbutz community, either in state politics or in various activities abroad. An average week in Yaari's life was described succinctly by his biographer:

> On Sundays he would receive visitors in Merhavia from other kibbutzim, read his mail and plan the rest of the week. On Mondays he would participate in the weekly meetings of the Kibbutz Haartzi Secretariat which took place in the Movement House in Merhavia. On Tuesdays he would either

---

8 Halamish, *The First Fifty Years*, 20–21.
9 Ibid., 131.
10 Aviva Halamish, *Meir Yaari—The Rebbe from Merhavia: The State Years* [in Hebrew] (Tel Aviv: Am Oved Publishers, 2013), 248–49.

write letters or visit various places all over the country. On Wednesdays he would stay in Tel Aviv where he participated in various official meetings and received representatives of kibbutzim. On Thursdays he took part in meetings of the Executive Committee of the Labor Union, the Histadrut. On Fridays he participated in the meetings of the Economy Committee in Haifa. Even on Saturdays he would do some work in his Merhavia home.[11]

Whereas ordinary members of the kibbutz lived and toiled in quite Spartan conditions, Yaari enjoyed all sorts of amenities while living in Tel Aviv and Jerusalem and especially during his frequent missions and stays abroad. While in Israel, he was chauffeured in a brand-new Chrysler, which in those days was considered a great luxury. He also spent time in various sanatoriums in Europe, due to his health problems. Criticism and remarks on his behavior from the family or the kibbutz would be met with great irritation. Yaari also had a streak of suspiciousness and complained of his isolation. In one of his letters to Anda, he spoke of himself as "a lonely, anxious and sick man."[12]

Even as a young man, Yaari showed tendencies toward leadership; these in time became increasingly pronounced. He was good in discussions and polemics and never forgot or forgave those who stood up to him. He was also known for his stubbornness. From quite an early age, he noticeably avoided cultivating close and intimate friends. People detected an authoritarian tendency in his social and political behavior as well as within his own family. According to his biographer, "Yaari tended to encourage attitudes which bordered on a personality cult."[13] Yaari was able to lead Hashomer Hatzair for decades, thanks to his personal charisma, the firmness of his ideological stance, and his organizational abilities.[14]

Zvi Vardi died five years before my arrival in Merhavia. At the time, I wasn't aware that Beit Zvi—the cultural center completed during my stay in the kibbutz—had been named after him. And it was only years later that I learned that Dina, one of the Gefen girls, was his daughter.

---

11 Halamish, *The First Fifty Years*, 233.
12 Halamish, *The Rebbe from Merhavia*, 97–98, 246–49.
13 Halamish, *The First Fifty Years*, 307.
14 Halamish, *The Rebbe from Merhavia*, 273.

Zvi Vardi, whose original name was Hersh Rosenkrantz, was in many ways the opposite of Meir Yaari. Born in eastern Galicia in 1905, he was seven years Yaari's junior. He arrived in Merhavia with the founders of the kibbutz in 1929. Zvi married Lina around that time. They had three daughters. Zvi's father and mother were among the few elderly parents who lived in Merhavia, and everybody referred to them as Sabba and Savta Rosenkrantz—Grandpa and Grandma Rosenkrantz.

Zvi loved people, and people loved him. He, too, was active at times outside his native kibbutz, but he was always regarded as a man whose priorities were inside, rather than outside, Merhavia. He was never selfish or egocentric, and he had a sense of humor. Whereas Yaari in time grew increasingly aloof, Zvi's most significant trait was camaraderie.[15] He always welcomed the new arrivals in the kibbutz and tried to make their absorption easier. Thus, a year after the arrival of the Neta group from Nazi-occupied Slovakia and Transylvania, Vardi openly apologized to them: "When you'd arrived a year ago you were barely given a greeting. Your expectations to continue your schooling went unfulfilled and you were thrown right away into daily work."[16] He warmly welcomed two Tehran Children who had escaped Nazi-occupied Poland and "arrived in Merhavia on Passover eve, in April 1943."[17]

Vardi's humane personality is clearly revealed in his correspondence with Shlomit, his firstborn daughter, who as a teenager lived and studied in Mishmar Haemek. He was always eager to share his thoughts and emotions with her and encouraged her to do the same: "My lovely Shlomit, you should never be ashamed of your emotions. You should always allow for warm feelings, for kindness and even for pleasure. One should never hide behind a rough façade. We should air our opinions and emotions. We should be humane."[18] In another letter, in which he discussed his daughter's peer group, he advised Shlomit, "look for the good, both within yourself and among your peers. Do not forget sports, reading, singing—things that add joy to your life." On the subject of relations between members of the kibbutz Vardi was quite outspoken: "I detest people who pry into the soul of the other to find defects and who always spread their suspicions around." He criticized the behavior of some members

---

15 Cnaani, *Sefer Merhavia*, 344–45.
16 Zvi Vardi, *Orhot Hevra* [in Hebrew] (Merhavia: Sifriat Hapoalim Publishers, 1946), 176.
17 Vardi, *Orhot Hevra*, 180.
18 Ibid., 190–91.

of the 1941 group: "I have detected among them a disregard for the other, a lack of empathy and at times even a mockery of those who have failed."[19]

Zvi Vardi died in October 1945 at the age of forty. During the last years of his life, he was ill. Still, most of the time he did not allow his increasing health problems to affect those around him. Only during his last few months did he speak openly about his suffering with his wife and his oldest daughter. He did not want to sadden his parents. In a letter he wrote them in Yiddish in March 1945 from Beilinson Hospital, he assured them, "I feel quite well."[20]

I have scant memories of Shlomit Aluma from my days in Merhavia. I associate her only as someone who played the *halil*—the recorder. Decades later, I found her name in numerous files in the Merhavia Archive. Interviews she recorded with the kibbutz founders helped me to understand the community in which she had spent her entire life and which I experienced for a short time. When I last saw her, she was already in her eighties and could barely communicate. I tried to tell her how useful her interviews were for my work. I'm not sure whether she could understand me.

Shlomit Aluma, the first-born daughter of Zvi Vardi, speaks, in the notes I found in the archive, of her childhood in Merhavia: "The wider contours of my childhood were the surrounding mountains and the Valley. Somewhat closer were Mount Gilboa and Giv'at Hamoreh." Then she zooms in on the kibbutz and its yard, the *khatser*:

> This was the epicenter of our existence, Merhavia's historic quadrangle. Those very special stone houses and that long building, with its arched portals. In the very center of the quadrangle was the *khatser*. Our childhood years were woven into that place. It was a shining white space, glimmering in the heat of the day. We, the children, tapped barefoot on the white dust that had no trace of shade. It burnt our feet. That burning sensation has remained with me for life. The yard glimmered in the moonlight as well, with a surreal white color, like that of the moon. We were born into that yard. That yard was the Beginning, was Creation.[21]

---

19 Ibid., 194.
20 Ibid., 215.
21 Shlomit Aluma, Merhavia Archive.

❋❋❋

My personal memories of Merhavia are few but quite vivid. Unlike most of the immigrant youngsters who joined kibbutzim in groups, I arrived alone and was placed in the Merhavia boarding school. Why? First, my aunt Pnina and her husband Shaya were among the founders of kibbutz Merhavia; and second, I actually knew some Hebrew from my school days in Lodz. My peer group in the boarding school was Gefen; it consisted of some twenty boys and girls, aged fourteen to fifteen. I was one of the oldest. I lived and studied with these boys and girls each and every day. Although formally we were all equals, I recall an informal status distinction within the Gefen group. On top were the "leaders": the two or three boys born to founder parents in Merhavia, who were the most developed, physically and mentally. They were also the first to have girlfriends, which made quite an impression on me. Next were all those whose parents were veteran kibbutz members. Then came the yaldei khutz: the "outside children," mostly sabras, with families living in various places in Israel. Immigrant boys and girls like me were referred to as "yaldei gola": "diaspora children." I was actually in a rather unique situation: although I had arrived from the *gola*—the diaspora—I had close family members in the kibbutz. There were three or four girls in Gefen, child survivors from Poland, who had joined the group at a younger age a few years before my arrival. They looked and acted like sabras. Each had a foster family in the kibbutz.

When I arrived in Merhavia, the local boarding school was fairly new. It had opened just a few years earlier. The rooms in our rectangular, one-story building were clean and cheerful. I quickly adapted myself to the new environment—outwardly, at least. My appearance was one of the first things to change. I was issued the standard kibbutz clothing: underwear, socks, pants, shirts, a sweater, an army-style jacket, and a *kova tembel*—the "fool's hat," to protect my head from the sun. I was assigned a room with three other members of the group: one boy and two girls. The boy's name was Gideon, a tall-ish youngster; there was a girl, Bela, and another—Batya. Gideon Weiss was a yeled khutz from Haifa; Bela, a child survivor from Poland. She looked and acted like a tough sabra. Batya was a Yemenite girl from Rehovot. The boys' beds were set against the wall on the right, and the girls' on the left. It was the first time that I'd ever lived or slept with strangers. This was something completely new to me, both difficult and exciting. The dressing and undressing of the girls aroused me. I stared furtively at their firm young breasts. I recall one hot and oppressive summer night. I couldn't fall asleep. The coolest place in the room was the tile floor. I got off my bed and lay down on the floor. Then I realized that big-breasted and shrill-voiced Bela was lying right beside me. I ached to touch her but was scared to do it. Another erotic memory is associated with the communal shower. When I joined Gefen, at least some of the girls and boys still showered together. I wasn't one of them. One afternoon I returned to the shower room in order to pick up my watch, which I may have forgotten intentionally. I was stunned. Gorgeous Abigail, with her beautiful chestnut colored braids stood there completely naked. Still another exciting sight etched in my memory were the girls' shorts, which revealed their alluring, sun-burnt thighs.

I had the good fortune to come across an interview in the Merhavia Archive conducted with Avraham Goren, who was appointed as Gefen's homeroom teacher in 1952—a year after I'd left Merhavia.[22] His recollections of my peer group are vivid and insightful. They helped me understand the mentality of those times. The years 1952–54 were perhaps the high point of admiration of Stalinist Russia by the Israeli Left, including the kibbutzim of Hashomer Hatzair. "We believed in the idea of Revolution and of 'purging the enemies.' We used Soviet-Russian history books translated into Hebrew. We regarded them as the words of God." This was also the time when the Gefen adolescents were supposed to receive the *semel bogrim*—the coveted emblem of becoming a senior member of the Hashomer Hatzair youth movement. The semel bogrim emblems were granted in the kibbutzim toward the end of the eleventh grade. In the case of Gefen, this rite of passage was to happen in the spring of 1953. The long-anticipated ceremony was preceded by months of discussions and preparations. Each member of the kvutza underwent a painful process of peer evaluation and self-criticism. Goren said, "this was a very tough experience, some people confessed their 'sins' and cried. I was alarmed by one of the girls, who ran out to the railroad tracks. Even such people as Ezra and Yoel identified with this kind of group pressure. Ehud was accused of not being sufficiently Movement-oriented. Ada apologized for being too close to her mother."

Menashke, Menahem Naveh, joined Gefen after I left. He was a rather small and thin city boy. He recalled the peer group meetings most vividly decades later: "Those discussions were tough and painful. They caused me such anxiety that I could hardly walk to the place they'd been held. I confessed and reported my sins. It was like lying on a psychiatrist's coach and being taken

---

22 Interview of Avraham Goren by Shlomit Aluma-Vardi, 1990, Merhavia Archive.

apart by eighteen people." Menashke was denied the semel bogrim. "I watched the ceremony from the other side of the fence and felt like a leper."[23]

At the same time, according to Goren, Gefen was one of the most impressive peer groups in the Merhavia boarding school. Its members were noted for their studiousness and for their serious and responsible attitudes toward various group activities. Goren remarks that one of the recurring problems within many peer groups was that of the yaldei khutz who arrived from time to time from the cities. At times, as much as half of each peer group consisted of outsiders. This problem affected Gefen, too.[24]

I'm sorry that Goren wasn't my teacher. Of the teachers I had, those whom I recall best were Eliezer and "Bozhik." Eliezer Reich taught us literature. Never pausing for a minute, he would pace about the class with great energy. When teaching poetry, he would recite the verses dramatically. He even arranged a competition to memorize some poems of Bialik. The winner was Arie Dagan, who recited from memory all the verses of "Hamatmid." "Bozhik," whose real name was Avraham Talmi, was our music teacher. I fondly recall his course in classical music. Some of those pieces I can identify to this day. He also taught us to play the mandolin, which I enjoyed very much. I recently learned that "Bozhik" passed away a few years ago at the age of ninety-five.

One of my worst memories from Merhavia has to do with nicknaming. It didn't matter that others in my kvutza were called by nicknames too. Gideon, my only close friend and roommate, was "Mifrasi," Flap-Ears; another boy of German origin was "Aschloch," Asshole. My nickname was "Skirki," which had no explicit meaning. I was told that before I'd arrived there was a boy in the kibbutz, a yeled gola whom I resembled, and that had been his nickname. For me "Skirki" clearly meant something unpleasant and derogatory. I do not recall that the "leaders" in the group, Arie and Ezra, were ever called by nicknames.

I don't remember the details of my decision to leave Merhavia. I am sure, however, that the main reason was that I could not expect to continue my education beyond high school: the kibbutz boarding school did not offer a matriculation exam. The prevailing attitude in Merhavia and throughout the movement at that time was negative with respect to higher education. I was not surprised when, decades later, I stumbled on a quote from Meir Yaari, man number one in the Kibbutz Haartzi movement and Merhavia's father figure, to the effect that "university-type education is not for us."[25]

---

23 Menachem Naveh, "No Rite of Passage for Menashke," 2002, Gefen File, Merhavia Archive.
24 Interview of Avraham Goren.
25 Halamish, *The First Fifty Years*, 173.

My memories of Merhavia are complex and at times contradictory. I have always regarded Merhavia as some sort of "unfinished business." For decades, I never really went back there. Although I did visit my aunt Pnina from time to time on the kibbutz, I was always careful not to show myself in public, and I never met with any member of my kvutza. The first time I consciously faced the issue of Merhavia was in the late 1980s, during the Demjaniuk trial. As a specialist in Ukrainian-Jewish relations, I was interviewed for *Al Hamishmar* by Sheli Yakhimovitch. This newspaper was read by the people of the Kibbutz Haartzi and Hashomer Hatzair, and I knew, of course, that it would be read in Merhavia, too. I doubt whether I would have made any comments regarding my personal connection with the kibbutz if my aunt Pnina had still been alive. But while discussing the wider context of Ukrainian-Jewish relations and Ukrainian attitudes towards Jews during the Holocaust, I decided on the spur of the moment to "get even" with Merhavia. Sheli Yakhimovitch, a young journalist who in time would become a central figure in Israeli politics, reported that "Professor Redlich, whose life was saved by a Ukrainian woman, does not nourish bad memories of Ukrainians. Instead he associates his bad memories with kibbutz Merhavia. He asserts that the year he spent there was a kind of shock treatment for him. It is there that he sensed his otherness. Nobody spoke with him about those terrible years of the war and the Holocaust."[26]

It is quite true that, emotionally, I felt better in Tanka's poor peasant household than I did years later among my Israeli peers in kibbutz Merhavia. Of course I was fully aware of the explosive quality of such a comparison. Two weeks later, a letter relating to the interview by an old-timer from another Hashomer Hatzair kibbutz was published in *Al Hamishmar*. It was an all-out attack on my statements: a mixture of criticism, cynicism, and contempt.[27] A few other letters from readers reacting to the interview were published in the following weeks, and then, toward the end of May, came a lengthy letter from Merhavia signed by Yaakov Shutzberg, one of the kibbutz founders. "When the boy Shimon Redlich came to Israel he was treated with the utmost hospitality in his aunt's house in Merhavia. His peers at that time and members of our kibbutz today recall that he was treated well. They even remember that he himself felt good. They were both surprised and upset by the interview." Shutzberg suggested that I be brave, admit my mistakes and apologize. "Thus will he atone for his sin."[28]

---

26 Sheli Yakhimovitch, *Al Hamishmar,* April 17, 1987.
27 Yehezkel Avni, "Who Should Be Forgiven And Who Shouldn't," *Al Hamishmar,* April 30, 1987.
28 Yaakov Shutzberg, "Was It a Shock Treatment for the Professor?," *Al Hamishmar,* May 29, 1987.

Around that time I also received a personal note from Yoel Mintzer, a one-time member of my group. His attitude differed completely from Shutzberg's. He seemed to understand and even to empathize. He recalled that there was, indeed, a "trampling of the Other" in those days, and he understood very well my "unfinished business" with Merhavia.[29] Another member of my group, Ezra Tsamri, had a similar reaction. When I interviewed him he distinctly recalled that "they didn't treat you well. I have no idea why."[30] These assorted memories from close to forty years after my stay in Merhavia are indicative both of the attitudes that prevailed there in the early 1950s, and of the sharply differing perceptions of that past.

When I interviewed some members of the kibbutz I kept asking them about their impressions of Yaakov "Janek" Shutzberg. A member of the 1941 group, Lusiek Grol, who also served as kibbutz secretary for several years, told me that, "Janek was a very active person and tried for years to shape the nature of Merhavia. He did have a 'Stalinist' and egocentric mentality. He was widely known for expressions like 'are you telling me?' and 'I'm sure I know (about it) much better than you.'"[31]

I returned to Merhavia in March 2009. It was no longer a kibbutz in the old sense of the word. It was a pale imitation of the thriving place that lives on in my memory. It was now bleak and neglected. The pavement was cracked. Gone were the lawns with the colorful flowers. The khadar haokhel, once the most impressive building in Merhavia, had been turned into a warehouse. The low-roofed, pleasant building of the boarding school, where I'd lived and studied, had become a shabby *ulpan*, an immigrants' dormitory. I was sad and glad at the same time. And the feelings of resentment left me.

Yoel Mintzer was the first person I contacted, and he was my host during that first visit. He would become my most significant contact in Merhavia, which, like numerous other kibbutzim, had undergone the difficult and painful process of privatization. His wife, Ruthi, a few years younger than he, is a therapist, and she let me sleep over in her office-studio. It turned out that her late father, Yitzhak Heruti, had been my aunt Pnina's next-door neighbor for many years. Ezra Tsamri was likewise very pleasant and confiding. He showed me his many works of art in which he had composed scenes and landscapes by pasting colorful patches of cloth on canvas, many with representations of kibbutz life

---

29 Shimon Redlich, "The Ability to Listen," *Al Hamishmar*, June 12, 1987.
30 Ezra Tsamri, interview by author, Merhavia, May 11, 2009.
31 Lusiek Grol, interview by author, Merhavia, August 7, 2009.

as it once was. A copy of one such work, showing at its center Merhavia's main yard, *hakhatser hagdola*, now adorns my study.

Esther, Ezra's wife, was one of the four survivor girls who joined Gefen a year after the war. When I met her in 1950, she was Ezra's girlfriend. We never spoke then about our common past in Poland. Now we embraced. I felt a certain affinity between us as child survivors. I also learned to my utter surprise that a younger branch of their family is orthodox and lives in Jerusalem. The relations between them are excellent. It was during this first visit that I started interviewing people and looking into the Merhavia Archive. During work breaks I went for coffee in the nearby coffee shop and was pleasantly surprised to learn that it was owned and run by Ada's family. Ada Fleisher was once a member of Gefen. When they phoned her and told her about the guest, she came running out to greet me.

One of the files that interested me most in the Merhavia Archive was labeled "Sikhot Kibbutz": the general assembly meetings. I was eager to learn what was being discussed during the time I was there. An examination of the general assembly minutes throughout 1950 reveals concern with ideological and political issues, along with specific local problems. One of the issues raised on February 20, 1950, was whether the *Mapam* party—the hard left, with which the Kibbutz Haartzi and Hashomer Hatzair were affiliated—should join a government dominated by Ben-Gurion's moderate-left *Mapai* party. Lusiek Grol of the 1941 group argued that Mapam should join only if it could have an impact as a "socialist element" within the coalition. Another subject concerned the construction of a *shikun vatikim*—a quarter for the old-time residents of Merhavia. Still another mundane matter was that of showers for the youngsters in the dormitory. The government-composition issue came up again two days later. Questions of ideological unity—*kolektiviut raayonit*—in politics and of the proper class approach to education were also raised at that meeting. Ryszard Weintraub, one of the old-timers, spoke out against the dangers of deviation from the movement's left-wing positions. The names of Marx and Lenin came up in the course of these discussions.[32]

The wishes of certain families or individual members to leave the kibbutz were the occasion of heated arguments. These were highly personal matters on

---

32 The General Assembly File, Merhavia Archive.

which any participant in the assembly could voice his opinion. Thus, the wish of Yael and Zeev to leave Merhavia was discussed by the assembly in mid-April 1950. Perhaps a few direct quotations can best portray the arguments as well as the tone of that meeting. Tuvia Yaari: "Difficulties concerning work assignments cannot be used as an excuse for leaving. They [Yael and Zeev] arrived here with a youth-group and the kibbutz has invested a good deal in them. We should, in my opinion, purge the kibbutz and end this business once and for all." Husia Mintzer: "I don't like this lighthearted attitude. This is an extremely serious matter we are dealing with. Tuvia's approach will lead us nowhere. Each person leaving the kibbutz is like a brick removed from its foundation. The only way is to convince people that by leaving they would harm both the kibbutz and themselves." Janek Shutzberg: "Those who leave the kibbutz are deserters from a battlefield. Some members have gone through crisis situations in the past but they did not leave. We have not managed to maintain the right attitude towards the kibbutz. We should learn a lesson from this case." Shlomit Vardi: "Preaching and lashing out isn't the answer. We need to try to keep these people within the kibbutz. It seems that our generation is less attached to the kibbutz than those who invested everything they had in it." Ryszard: "It seems to me that the real problem is not this or that work assignment. It is basically a problem of whether one has roots within the kibbutz."[33]

A number of the assemblies in the early summer of 1950 discuss the upcoming movement council: *moetset hatnuah*. The general tone on the subject of the significance of the kibbutzim within Israeli society at large was rather downbeat. It was pointed out that the size of the kibbutz population relative to the country's overall population was steadily decreasing and that there was a sense of laxity. Meir Yaari spoke of the necessity of holding Hashomer Hatzair activities among young immigrants so as to beef up the kibbutz population. Buma Yassur, as usual, used Marxist terminology to characterize his view of contemporary Israeli society: "The class conflict has increased. The bourgeoisie attempts to conquer new positions." Tzvia N. pointed out that although there was a need to attract new immigrants, the suggestion that some of them should be invited for the Passover Seder in Merhavia was being met by "a general opposition." Ben-Gurion's critique of the kibbutzim with respect to the absorption of immigrants provoked an extremely heated exchange of views. The person in charge of writing up the minutes commented, "Peri gets very irritated, Kuba Fleisher tries to calm things down, Tuvia Yaari tries to joke, Yuzhi

---

33 Ibid.

just smiles." During one of the subsequent meetings, Kuba Riftin of Mishmar Haemek—a leader of the radical leftist wing of the Kibbutz Haartzi—spoke of the necessity for class struggle, ideological cohesiveness, and ideological collectivism. He criticized the lack of a militant spirit in the kibbutz movement.[34]

Another issue raised several times that summer concerned Buma Yassur. The discussion, the arguments, and the final outcome reflected the relations between the movement and one of its kibbutzim: in this case, Merhavia. The movement decided that Buma should work for a while at its center in Tel Aviv; Merhavia demanded that he work within the kibbutz. Moshe Man argued that only a person who has been sufficiently rooted in the kibbutz could do work outside the collective, and that this wasn't the case with Buma. He further argued that it was undesirable to turn kibbutz members into movement functionaries. Shlomit Vardi was apparently the only one to ask the assembly to take into account the personal and humane aspect of Buma's work for the movement: "We should consider Hava (Buma's wife), a new kibbutz member, who hasn't made close friends yet; so that it would be extremely difficult for her if she is left here alone."[35]

The most widely sounded argument against Buma working outside the kibbutz was the severe shortage of manpower in Merhavia. The assembly of July 4, 1950, decided almost unanimously to reject the demand of the movement. The issue got raised again in late August. This time there were differences of opinion. Some speakers stuck to the previous decision. Others were ready to comply with the movement's request. Among them were Janek Shutzberg, Lusiek Grol, and Meir Yaari. Of thirty-seven participants, twenty voted to let Buma work at the movement center on condition that another member of Merhavia working there would be freed up for work in the kibbutz. Seventeen voted, under duress, to comply with the movement's request. As the date for Buma's appointment outside the kibbutz approached, still another assembly, in mid-September 1950, reversed the previous decisions. Meir Yaari, Janek Shutzberg, Ryszard Weintraub, and Buma Yassur himself strongly opposed Merhavia's clash with the movement. The vote was twenty-three in favor of Buma working for the movement, thirteen opposed. The minutes of the meeting ended with, "Final decision: Buma goes to work for the Movement."[36]

---

34 Ibid.
35 Ibid.
36 Ibid.

One of the issues raised in the assembly in the fall of 1950 was David Zamir's wish to leave Merhavia and to join kibbutz Geva, a nearby kibbutz not affiliated with the Kibbutz Haartzi. Although Zamir had settled in Merhavia a few years after the initial group, he was considered a veteran. This was probably why his wish to depart evoked such strong reactions. Zamir's reasons for wanting to leave were a mixture of personal and ideological grievances. Husia Mintzer was quite emotional about the prospect of Zamir and his family leaving Merhavia. He concluded his argumentation with a direct appeal: "Zamir, please reconsider!" Eliezer Peri, in his appeal, presented Zamir's prospective exit as a "parting from the common road" and as an act of "alienation." He also spoke of the overall need to bolster political vigilance and ideological collectivism. Zamir, in a lengthy response, spoke about his frustration with his work. He also had criticisms of the prevailing ideology and the movement's politics. He lamented the lack of tolerance in Merhavia, as opposed to kibbutz Geva where "they have seven *Mapam* members who are treated with respect." Following a heated and loud debate, Zamir was granted a leave of three months to make up his mind. He apparently did move to Geva for some time, but eventually returned to Merhavia. He ended up in the least respected work category, as a *pkak*—plug—doing short-term jobs of various sorts. In kibbutz society he seemed the odd man out.[37]

A case study conducted by an American anthropologist in Merhavia in the mid-1960s dealt with "Stigma and Morality." It revolved around Zamir's son Uzi. I have a vague recollection of Uzi, who was in Shalhevet, the senior group in the boarding school during my time. He was a lanky youngster with a limp. I never exchanged a word with him, but his name came up during my interviews. I was told that the children of his peer group used to help him due to his physical handicap. According to Jetka, who was the metapelet—nursery-school teacher—of Uzi's peer group, "Uzi was the youngest and already then he had a problem with his legs. The kids would always help him tie his shoelaces."[38]

As an adolescent he still seemed to "belong," despite his disability. In time, however, his otherness became increasingly pronounced. By the mid-sixties, Uzi's social estrangement was apparent to all. He differed from his peer-group both physically and mentally. He never served in the army. Like other Shalhevet members, he did become in time a full member of the kibbutz. But he had fewer and fewer interactions with his peers. He spent most of his free time with his

---

37 Ibid.
38 Jetka Goldblat, video interview, in author's possession.

parents. His mother died in 1957 and his father did not remarry. Uzi failed at several types of kibbutz work, and was finally assigned to work in residential gardening, one of the easiest jobs, usually given to women. Only rarely was he invited to private parties and other intimate meetings of his peers. There were also rumors about Uzi's sexual improprieties. Zamir, the father, was stigmatized, too. People described the father as "nervous," "stupid," "a slob," "an idiot." He became the butt of jokes. People avoided sitting near him during meals. Yet there were also kibbutz members who referred to him as an "idealist."[39]

The stigmatization of Uzi and his father came to a head when Uzi announced his wish to marry a young woman from an immigrant family from Iraq. The issue was brought to the general assembly, where it was maintained that the woman was "not kibbutz material" and that "the mood of the community" was against their living in Merhavia. There were allusions to her origin, illiteracy, ugliness. Some of Uzi's young female peers objected to the possibility of sitting together with that woman during breast-feeding sessions. Uzi could continue his work on the kibbutz, it was suggested, but the couple would have to live somewhere else nearby. At the same time, however, the kibbutz was ready, in the event of the death of Uzi or his future wife, to take in the surviving mate and their children. The story of Uzi brings out the kibbutz's practices of ostracization and stigmatization on the one hand and the collective's sense of moral obligation to its members on the other.[40]

As for the general assembly in Merhavia, its significance seems to have been eroding already during my time there. By the early 1960s, attendance had become a serious problem, especially among the younger generation.[41]

To gain a better understanding of what kibbutz Merhavia was like in the years I was there, I, along with examining the personal files, also interviewed some of the surviving members.

Yitzhak Heruti, usually just referred to as "Heruti," and his wife, Hanka, were neighbors of my aunt Pnina. They lived in one of the newly built houses

---

39 Terrence M. S. Evens, "Stigma and Morality in a Kibbutz," in *A Composite Portrait of Israel*, ed. Emmanuel Marx (New York: Academic Press, 1980), chapter 8.
40 Evens, "Stigma and Morality"; personal communication by Yoel Mintzer.
41 T. M. S. Evens, *Two Kinds of Rationality: Kibbutz Democracy and Generational Conflict* (Minneapolis: University of Minnesota Press, 1995), 32, 52.

for the *vatikim*—the old-timers. I never knew their personal stories. I learned about them only by studying their files in the Merhavia Archive.

Yitzhak Heruti was born in Sambor, southwest of Lviv, in 1905. His father was a petty merchant. The everyday language in their family was Yiddish, though the father spoke German as well. Heruti was the youngest child. "Father cared very much about our education. Almost all my older siblings were sent to study in Vienna," Heruti recalled. The most popular Zionist youth movement in Sambor was Hashomer Hatzair. Young Heruti was a member and even served for a while as its *Rosh Ken*—branch leader. He immigrated to Palestine in 1926 and soon joined the group that would, three years later, turn into kibbutz Merhavia. Besides taking on physical labor assignments of all kinds, Heruti led youth activities and was involved in the beginnings of Hashomer Hatzair in Mandatory Palestine, mainly in Tel Aviv. It was in the framework of such extensive work with youth that his path crossed with that of his future wife, Hanka. Hanka wrote Heruti in October 1929, "I am very glad to hear about your wish to continue working with youth groups." She also encouraged him to start meeting high-school students.[42]

Heruti had been friendly with a close friend of Hanka, Efratia Margalit. Efratia wrote from Vienna in 1931 to her sister Sarah in Tel Aviv, advising her to get acquainted "with my good friend Heruti from Merhavia and seek his companionship and advice."[43] The next day she wrote her brother Yig'al "to convey my regards to all our brethren and sisters in the Tel Aviv *ken* of Hashomer Hatzair as well as to Heruti. I know him well. He is very successful in his work—our work."[44] Heruti, who for a while headed the first branch of Hashomer Hatzair in Tel Aviv, was one of the founders of the Hashomer Hatzair youth movement in Palestine. He was also instrumental in promoting and organizing a group of young men and women of Hashomer Hatzair, most of them high-school graduates from Tel Aviv, who settled in Merhavia in 1941.

Hanka Weinberg was born in Lodz in 1909 and attended the local Hebrew high school. Its students also included Zvi Vardi and Zvi Lurie, who would

---

42 Chana to Heruti, October 13, 1929, Heruti File, Merhavia Archive.
43 "Letter from Efratia to Sarah, July 22, 1931," in *Efratia Gitai: Correspondence, 1929–1994* [in Hebrew], ed. Rivka Gitai (Tel Aviv: Miskal Publishers, 2011), 65.
44 "Letter from Efratia to Yig'al, July 23, 1931," in *Efratia Gitai*, 67.

in time become prominent members of the Kibbutz Haartzi movement in Palestine. The future Yiddish actor and comedian Israel Schumacher was also a graduate of that high school. The Weinbergs immigrated to Palestine in 1925 and settled in Tel Aviv. Hanka continued her secondary education at the prestigious Herzliyah High School. She graduated in 1928. Hanka was not only a top-ranking student but was also very active socially and ideologically. Those who knew her at that time always remembered her as a very special person. Yona Golan from Mishmar Haemek wrote half a century later,

> Hanka was at one and the same time a shy and outstanding young woman. In spite of being physically slight, she was blessed with a strong personality. She always knew what she wanted. There was also something mysterious about her. One summer she disappeared and told no one about her whereabouts. Only later did it emerge that she had joined a Hashomer Hatzair group in Bat-Galim, the group which later would become kibbutz Merhavia.[45]

Another friend of Hanka from her Herzliyah days wrote years afterward that "she had a well-sculpted face, big blue eyes with a shade of grey, and curly hair that slid across her shoulders. She was beautiful and we all fell in love with her." Hanka soon became a revered counselor of a youth group. "With a little harmonica in her mouth she would dance tirelessly and cause others to dance."[46] A personal note by Hanka vividly portrays the prevailing mood among her young friends in the Tel Aviv of the 1920s: "A spirit of friendship permeated us all. People made up with each other after quarrels and kissed each other freely."[47]

Hanka made her first contact with the founders of Merhavia during the summer of 1928, a year before they settled in the Valley. She was then nineteen and Heruti, twenty-three. At the time, the future settlers were still living in Bat Galim near Haifa and were working in the vicinity. Heruti recalled, "I saw her for the first time when we returned from our work draining the Kishon stream. We were all stained with mud. They told us that a beautiful girl had arrived and that all the young men are mad about her." Hanka joined the group and worked with them day after day in the most challenging kinds of labor: "In the evenings she joined us in counseling the Haifa-based Hanoar Haoved and Hashomer

---

45 Yona Golan-Ben Yaakov, "About Hanka Weinberg," *Mishmar Haemek*, February 10, 1986, Heruti File.
46 Efratia Gitai, "About Hanka Heruti-Weinberg," n.d., Heruti File.
47 Hanka Weinberg, personal note, 1928, Heruti File.

Hatzair youth groups. That was the beginning of our friendship." Young Hanka was liked and respected. She was even allowed to join the *sihat haverim*—the collective's general assembly. She was principled, straightforward, and outspoken. Some people didn't like that: "Already then Hanka took a stand against harsh and extreme attitudes." Heruti recalls, "We know quite well how the kibbutz was in those first years. We used to literally 'dissect' a kibbutz member. And that's how they would 'dissect' Hanka years later, when she sought to work as a doctor. Within our kibbutz, then as well as now, some people see things only in black and white." As for Hanka, according to Heruti, "after that summer she returned to Tel Aviv deeply infected with the Hashomer Hatzair and the kibbutz virus."[48]

Then came Hanka's unusual mission to the Jewish community in Aden. She worked there with adults and with youth. Besides her formal activities, she assisted young Jewish girls who had been sexually abused. She would even host them in her own house. A few years after Hanka's death, a letter was found on her tombstone in the Merhavia cemetery. It was addressed to *Chana Hatsadika*—Chana the Righteous. One of the girls from Aden who had made *aliyah*—immigrated to Israel—wrote, "I constantly think of her: she comes to me in my dreams. I weep and remember what she had done for me. She was like a mother to me when I was 11 and 12 years old. She saved me and brought me into her house. She was an angel." The Yemenite woman left money in the envelope. Heruti used it to install a memorial candle fixture on Hanka's tombstone.[49]

It was during her stay in Aden that Hanka made up her mind to study medicine. A close friend recalls that, "though she had already decided to join the kibbutz when she went to Bat-Galim, Hanka planned to do it in her own way: she would join as a doctor." Hanka arrived in Vienna in 1931 but did not begin her medical studies right away. She first studied psychology and education. She came to Vienna with some of her Herzliyah schoolmates and friends, among them Efratia Margalit and Yemima Tchernovitz. Efratia confided in a letter that "we went to Vienna in order not to be parochial." Years later her son, Amos Gitai, the renowned Israeli film director, remarked about this group of young Jewish women from Palestine that "these women had no fear." Efratia had a distinct memory of Hanka from their Vienna days: "What drove her was her youthful curiosity, a thirst for culture, good theatre, concerts, hikes to the

---

48 Yitzhak Heruti, "About Hanka," Heruti File.
49 "Hanukka," unsigned letter, 1965, Heruti File.

Wiener Wald. She absorbed all of it like a sponge."[50] Hanka became active in the Vienna branch of Hashomer Hatzair and was always surrounded by young and educated people. Hanka and Efratia visited a Hashomer Hatzair youth camp in Hungary in August 1931: "They were very happy with us. We assisted them greatly on the topic of *Eretz Israel*. Hanka helped out in organizational affairs and I participated in discussions."[51] Just as had happened years earlier during her time in the Herzliyah high school, young men and women were drawn in by her endless energy and vitality.

The rise of fascism in Austria forced Hanka to leave Vienna and move to Switzerland. She continued her medical studies in Basel and became a doctor in 1938. Although she was offered a position and advancement there, Hanka returned to Palestine and settled in Merhavia.[52]

The landing in Merhavia was not an easy one. The bone of contention was her profession. Although some members, including Meir Yaari, supported Hanka's wish to be both a kibbutz member and a doctor, others opposed it. Despite being a physician, "she started out as a health worker. She cleaned showers and toilets. She was also assigned to work in the fields."[53] Dr. Erich Nassau, head of the children's department in the nearby Valley Hospital, invited Hanka to join his staff. The minutes of the general assembly meeting of July 1942 record quite a dramatic exchange of views concerning Hanka's request. Yaakov Tsamri supports Hanka: "I believe that while working as a doctor she will be able to maintain a close contact with the kibbutz." Husia Mintzer supports Tsamri's view, while Tuvia Yaari seems to be against it. Another participant, Yitzhak, is strongly against Hanka's working as a doctor "on principle." Shilek suggests that they vote on a proposition that "the kibbutz supports Hanka's work as a doctor." Out of forty-three members in attendance, forty vote for and three against.[54]

Hanka apparently felt hurt by this debate in spite of the overwhelming support she received. She spoke out during an assembly meeting in early August: "It is not a question of my career or my prestige. Whether intentionally

---

50 Efratia Gitai, "About Hanka," Heruti File; Maya Sela, "Interview with Amos Gitai," *Haaretz*, April 14, 2011.
51 Letter from Efratia to her father, in *Efratia Gitai*, 73.
52 Z. Shehory-Rubin, "Dr. Hanka Weinberg-Herouti: The Pediatrician from Merhavia—The First Woman Doctor 'Kibbutznik' in the Kibbutz Ha'artzi," *Harefuah: Journal of the Israel Medical Association* 154, no. 7 (July 2015): 460–63.
53 Gitai, "About Hanka."
54 General Assembly Meetings File, July 1942, Merhavia Archive.

or not, I've been hurt. There still remain some people who are demanding proof of my membership in the kibbutz. I've been part of the Movement for years, even before joining Merhavia. I protest the wish of these people to deny me the very content of my life. I demand that they tell me openly what my error has been and not whisper about it to one another." Zvi Vardi was unequivocal on the matter: "The stand of the kibbutz regarding Hanka's work has been clearly stated by an overwhelming majority." Hanka wasn't satisfied: "I still see that some people see me differently than I perceive myself. I consider this a question of supreme significance. Such attitudes hurt."[55] Indeed, some staunch critics did not change their views for years. "The struggle against her right to work as a doctor never ceased," Heruti stated decades later. "It seems that some kibbutz members could never accept the fact that she had studied for a degree, that she was different."[56]

Through all the years in which she worked at Valley Hospital, Hanka was a well-liked and respected professional. Professor Erich Nassau held her in high esteem both for her work as a physician and for her medical research. He considered her his "best and most faithful worker."[57]

Heruti and Hanka's home in Merhavia was one of those open kibbutz households that often hosted guests from the "outside world." Heruti, who, among his various jobs and activities, was also an amateur theatre director, was friendly for many years with Orna Porat, the German-born Israeli actress. She and her Jewish husband, Yosef Proter-Porat, a senior figure in Israeli intelligence, were frequent guests in the Heruti home. So were the theater critic Dr. Haim Gamzou and his son Yosi. Another frequent visitor was the archeologist Pessah Bar-Adon, who lived nearby with his American wife, the author Dorothy Kahan. There was also the architect Munio Weinraub, who in his teenage years was a member of Hashomer Hatzair in Poland, and who later studied with the founders of the Bauhaus school of architecture in Germany. Munio was involved in architectural projects for several kibbutzim of the Kibbutz Haartzi, especially in Kfar Masarik, near Haifa, and he planned the expansion of Merhavia's khadar haokhel. Munio's wife, Efratia, was Hanka's classmate in the Herzliyah high school; they remained close friends. When Efratia was due to give birth in the fall of 1940 she went to stay with Hanka in Merhavia, and Hanka made the necessary arrangements at the nearby Valley Hospital. In a

---

55 General Assembly Meetings File, August 8, 1942, Merhavia Archive.
56 Amiram Cohen, "Dr. Hanka Heruti—A Sad Story," *Hadaf Hayarok*, Heruti File.
57 Dr. E. Nassau's letter to Hanka, March 2, 1961, Heruti File.

letter to her parents Efratia wrote, "I feel like a 'citizen' of Merhavia." Hanka and Heruti would often visit the Weinraubs in Haifa. Close ties between the families continued in later years, too, and the Weinraub boys, Gidi and Amos, also spent time at the Heruti's in Merhavia.⁵⁸

It seems that, starting in the 1920s and for the next few decades, close contacts were maintained between some members of the Kibbutz Haartzi kibbutzim and their personal and ideological friends in the cities. It was also natural for Hanka to maintain contacts with her medical colleagues, especially her close friends Dr. Yaakov Rothem and Dr. Shimon Brandstetter; the latter had also been a friend of Munio Weinraub from their Hashomer Hatzair days in Poland. Dr. Chaim Sheba was another of Hanka's acquaintances. "Hanka was the glue which held them all together."⁵⁹

Hanka fell ill in the late 1950s and died of cancer in early March 1961, on the eve of Purim, in Haifa's Rambam Hospital. Her ambivalent feelings toward Merhavia were expressed in her last wish. According to Heruti, "she asked that members of the kibbutz not accompany her to the Merhavia cemetery and that the funeral procession not pass through the kibbutz. She also asked that her burial not interfere with the kibbutz children's celebration of Purim."⁶⁰

Jetka Goldblat, another person from the founder's group, was a tough and highly opinionated individual. She was a close friend and next-door neighbor of my aunt Pnina. Like Pnina, she came originally from Brzezany, and also like Pnina, she was one of the founders of the kibbutz. Jetka never married. She worked for fifteen years in Merhavia's cowshed, one of the best in the country. She also worked as a children's nurse—a metapelet—which she described later in an interview:

> The parents at that time didn't get involved in the upbringing of the children at all and would spend very short periods of time with them. The kids were very happy to be with me. There were no problems whatsoever. Although I erred at times, I did possess two significant qualities: dedication and love. The children loved me. When arrangements were made to

---

58 Rivka Gitai, ed., *Efratia Gitai*, 119–24.
59 Ibid.; personal communication from Yoel Mintzer, October 4, 2015.
60 Cohen, "Dr. Hanka Heruti."

create the first grade, I was appointed as their *metapelet*. Everything went well. I survived in that job for ten years and then decided to quit.⁶¹

When reading the memoirs of Ruta Weintraub-Klein, the daughter of Ryszard Weintraub and the wife of Zvi Klein, I learned that Jetka had been quite harsh with some of the children. "Our *metapelet*, Jetka, used to spank me. When I didn't eat she spanked me. When I didn't speak up she spanked me. When I did speak up she spanked me as well. My very presence, apparently, annoyed her."⁶²

Lusiek Grol, of the 1941 hashlama, was the oldest member of the kibbutz whom I was able to interview. Rather short and neatly dressed, when I approached his house he was outside in his tiny garden, trimming roses.

Lusiek was born in 1920 in Drohobycz, in eastern Galicia, to an upper middle-class family. His parents spoke both Yiddish and Polish, but with him, they spoke only Polish. He studied in the local Polish high school, the gymnasium. One of his teachers was Bruno Schulz, who would later become famous as a writer and artist. Young Grol socialized comfortably with both Jews and Poles; one of his closest friends was a Polish student, a Communist. It was during his high-school days that he joined the Drohobycz branch of Hashomer Hatzair. Lusiek was eighteen when he arrived in Palestine to study at the Mikve Israel agricultural school, but he was soon asked by the Movement to work with the youth as an ideological instructor.⁶³

Lusiek had formed personal contacts with kibbutz Merhavia even before his arrival. A few of its founders had come from his hometown. Among them were his cousins, the Mintzer brothers, and Janek Shutzberg. Lusiek liked Merhavia. "The central yard with its stone houses was very impressive." Quite soon after settling there, Lusiek enlisted in the British Army and served in it for four years. He fought with the Jewish Brigade in Italy. Following the liberation of Poland, he met Holocaust survivors there, such as Abba Kovner, Vitka Kempner, and Rozka Korczak. With other soldiers of the brigade, Lusiek

---

61 Jetka Goldblat, video interview, in author's possession.
62 Ruta Weintraub-Klein, *Other Days* [in Hebrew] (Kibbutz Dalia: Maarechet Publishing House, 2002), 66.
63 Lusiek Grol, interview by author, Merhavia, August 2009.

traveled to Germany, to the Dachau and Mauthaussen internment camps, to assist in the *brichah* campaign to bring Jewish survivors to Palestine. "I was a young man of twenty five. My encounter with camp survivors was depressing. It was a shock. Initially they distrusted us. They wouldn't believe that we were going to bring them to Palestine. We had to convince them." Lusiek was one of those Jewish Brigade soldiers who stole weapons for the *Haganah* in France, Belgium, and Holland. During one of his leaves of absence from the army, in early 1943, he married Rachel, the daughter of Meir Yaari. It was only in the summer of 1946 that he returned home to Merhavia, where he went to work in the cowshed. After some time, he was dispatched again to France to work with Hashomer Hatzair youth. In the early 1960s, he studied for his PhD at the Sorbonne, specializing in political science and political philosophy. He published several books. Subsequently, Lusiek divided his work between Merhavia and Tel Aviv University.

I may have seen Tuvia Ruebner once or twice during my stay in Merhavia. I met him in person for the first time only a half-century later. In my mind, Tuvia's name has always been associated with a dramatic and tragic event that occurred during my first weeks in Israel. A bus traveling from Tel Aviv to Afula had an accident and was almost completely burnt. Tuvia's young wife, Ada—the mother of their infant girl—perished in that accident. Tuvia himself was severely burnt. People kept talking about it for weeks.

Tuvia Ruebner, who would in time become a leading Israeli poet, arrived in Merhavia as a seventeen-year-old youngster. He was born to an affluent Jewish family in Bratislava in 1924. His sister was born five years later. Tuvia's childhood and youth were quite contented and free of cares. Even when the shadow of Nazi Germany fell upon Slovakia, he still enjoyed life. As he later recalled, "I left for a Hashomer Hatzair summer camp in Banska Bistrica. We boys and girls had a wonderful time. I had some close friends there, I wrote poems and played the mandolin, I fell in love for the first time." Tuvia left Bratislava with a group of Zionist youngsters in April 1941, and—via Budapest, Constanza, Constantinople and Beirut—he reached Atlit in British Palestine. Just days later, the youngsters were already in Merhavia. Tuvia records his first encounter with the kibbutz: "We reached Merhavia on a terribly hot day. The temperature was close to 42 degrees Celsius. I'd never experienced such heat.

We got off the bus near Beit Hatnuah—The Movement Headquarters. Nearby we spotted a few dusty pine trees with a monkey chained to one of them." Tuvia tried to pet it and was rewarded with a vicious bite.[64]

The newcomers were quartered in the old dilapidated *khadar haokhel* and slept on the floor on mattresses stuffed with corn husks. Their personal effects were soon taken from them. "These were the high days of the '*komuna*'—the collective clothing principle. Our shirts, underwear and suits were confiscated and distributed among the kibbutz members. *Men darft zich tzugevoynen*, we were told in Yiddish: one needs to adjust.'"[65]

Tuvia's recollection was that people weren't friendly at all. "There was no human touch. They just expected us to work and assigned us the worst kind of labor." The kibbutz children called them "*pochkes*." One youngster in Tuvia's group was actually named Pochek, but the plural invented on the spot by local children was certainly derogatory. During our interview, I quoted to Tuvia a passage from his memoir in which he speaks negatively of some of the people in the kibbutz. He remarked that "there were indeed bad people among them. There was jealousy. Newcomers were usually exploited. Merhavia was known in the Movement for its bad human relations." When I asked Tuvia's wife, Galila, about her impressions on moving to Merhavia from her native kibbutz Ein Harod, she replied, "There was a great difference between them. In Ein Harod at that time there were already many gray heads. Not so in Merhavia. Ein Harod had a big heart. I did not find that here. There was a kind of Galician attitude in the air. What people said wasn't exactly what they meant. Every small place has some gossip. In Merhavia it was more malevolent—vicious."[66]

For Tuvia, there was also the unexpected, shocking encounter with the new landscapes, light, and colors. His childhood and youth had been spent close to meadows, forests, streams, rivers. "When I arrived here a scorching light hit me full in the face. All colors were wiped out during the day. It was only toward the evening that they started reappearing. Everything around me was gray and dusty."[67]

Tuvia also recalled the happy times in his early kibbutz life. "After a while I became a shepherd. I recall those contented moments during the grazing time in the spring. The sheep were quiet. The grass was tall and rich. One could just

---

64 Tuvia Ruebner, *Ein Langes Kurzes Leben* [in Hebrew] (Tel Aviv: Keshev Publishing House, 2006), 52.
65 Ibid.
66 Tuvia and Galila Ruebner, interview by author, Merhavia, August 2009.
67 Ruebner, *Ein Langes Kurzes Leben*, 89.

lay down, stretch out and sense the heat of the soil. Some kind of bond was born between me and that soil. It gave me a sense of security, of home." Later on he worked as librarian and teacher.

All along, Tuvia kept up meaningful contacts with Israeli writers and poets outside the kibbutz. He would meet with Avraham Shlonsky and would become a close friend of Leah Goldberg. Ludwig Strauss was older than Tuvia; Dan Pagis, younger. Both, like Tuvia, were steeped in German culture, literature, and poetry. Tuvia also developed a hobby: photography. His early work dates from 1948 and he was still taking photographs in his eighties.[68]

For years, Tuvia nourished memories of his family and particularly of his younger sister, all of whom perished in the Holocaust. Recollections of his sister kept appearing in various poems. One poem written on the occasion of a spring festival, the collective Passover dinner in the kibbutz dining hall, speaks of "the dining tables, the bright lights, signifying life. My sister rests, surrounded by flowers." She then turns into a goldfish; then a blackbird and then a cloud hovering over his life. On another occasion Tuvia confessed that for him his dead sister had become "the essence of all grief and mourning."[69]

Personal tragedies seemed to have dogged Tuvia throughout his life. Following the loss of his family in wartime Europe, he lost his young wife, Ada, a short time after the birth of their daughter. In a poem published sixty-three years afterward, Tuvia speaks to her: "How did you step out of the frame on my desk and awaken me to the dread of your death." In an earlier poem he had asked, "Who is she, whose daughter summons her mom." The memories and the grief continue. "She left us at dawn. Her night started then – at dawn."[70] Years later, his son, Moran, disappeared in South America. Tuvia confessed, "I've been in shock since Moran disappeared."[71]

I wondered about Tuvia's identity after sixty years of life on the kibbutz. He summed it up: "In Merhavia I've accepted to a certain extent the world around me but with some kind of inner resistance. My real life has been my poetry."[72]

---

68 Tuvia Ruebner, *Gam zot ra'u eynay* [in Hebrew] (Tel Aviv: Keshev Publishing House, 2007).
69 Tuvia Ruebner, *And Hastens to His Place, 1953–1989* [in Hebrew] (Tel Aviv: Sifriat Hapoalim Publishers, 1990), 17–19; Ruebner, *Ein Langes Kurzes Leben*, 7, 44, 56, 79; Edna Shabtai, "Since Their Son Disappeared," *Yediot Aharonot*, October 16, 1987, 45–46; Tuvia and Galila Ruebner, interview.
70 Tuvia Ruebner, *Last: 2011–2012* [in Hebrew] (Tel Aviv: Keshev Publishing House, 2013), 55; Ruebner, *And Hastens to His Place*, 59, 111.
71 Shabtai, "Since Their Son Disappeared," 45–46.
72 Ruebner, *Ein Langes Kurzes Leben*, 114; Tuvia and Galila Ruebner, interview.

✣ ✣ ✣

Zvi Klein came to Merhavia with the *Hahotrim* group, the one that arrived after Tuvia's. Zvi was born in Croatia in 1926 to an upper middle-class Jewish family. His name at the time was Peter. Three languages were spoken in his home: German, Hungarian, and Croatian. There was always a nanny in the house, usually Viennese. The family moved to Italian-ruled Dalmatia sometime in 1941, using forged identity papers. Zvi and his parents then spent two years living on several islands in the Adriatic Sea, which were then still under Italian rule. The war ended for them in British-liberated southern Italy. Zvi was then seventeen. Since Zvi and his father knew several languages and by then had also acquired some English, they worked as translators for the British. Around that time, they received certificates permitting them to relocate to Palestine. In the summer of 1944, Zvi boarded a Polish luxury liner, the *Stefan Batory*, with a destination of Alexandria. This was to be a turning point in his life. On the *Batory*, he met a group of young Zionists from Yugoslavia, soon to become the Hahotrim group. Zvi decided to join them. Zvi and his father did not have any prior Zionist background. "We weren't Zionists. We went to Palestine since that was the only place where we could go," Zvi said later. As for the youngsters from Yugoslavia, Zvi recalled that "they used to sit together, sing Israeli songs and say they are going to join a kibbutz. Following our arrival in the Atlit transit camp a man came to meet us. This was Shalom Lurie from Merhavia. He took us by bus to Haifa and then to Afula. A horse and carriage was waiting for us at the local bus station and took us to the kibbutz."[73]

A few young men and women joined the group over the next two years, and its number increased to twenty. Among them were a Romanian girl from Transnistria and two boys from Greece. Zvi recalls that some of the Hahotrim group brought their parents to live in the kibbutz, among them "Grandpa Fischer" and "Grandpa Fuerst." The group's "mother" was Sonya Levavi, one of the kibbutz founders and a specialist in raising chickens. She was also the real mother of Omana, the first child born in Merhavia. According to Zvi, most of his group eventually left the kibbutz. He was one of the few who remained. "I married a native Merhavia girl, the daughter of Ryszard Weintraub. Our romance came to its peak sometime in 1949, shortly after the end of the War of Independence. There was a big party in the dining hall. The most valuable wedding gift was two small kettles. We moved into our 'family room' in 1949."

---

73   Zvi Klein, interview by author, Merhavia, July 2009.

When I asked for his impressions of Merhavia in those years, Zvi responded that there was "a certain harshness, in an ideological as well as a personal sense. There was also some jealousy." The kibbutz, for example, was opposed to higher education, and several young people left because of this attitude. "Most of the kibbutz founders came from small towns and poor families. There was also gossip. I assume that a Hungarian kibbutz or a kibbutz of Yekkes would differ from a kibbutz of Galitzianers. And although the founders were Galitzianers, the kibbutz became a very heterogeneous community. Various groups and individuals settled there over time."[74]

We also discussed the problem of leaving the kibbutz: "When somebody decided to leave in those days, they'd tear him to pieces. The person would have to endure harsh criticism in front of everybody in the Assembly. There would be preaching and moralizing and accusations of treachery. Some of the most vociferous kibbutz members on such occasions were Tuvia Yaari and Janek Shutzberg."[75]

Yaakov and Aharon Shabtai joined Merhavia as individuals. They were born to a working-class family in Tel Aviv. Both attended the same elementary school and were members of the same youth movement, Hashomer Hatzair. It was through the movement and its central branch in Tel Aviv—the *ken-merkaz*—that they ended up, at least for part of their lives, in kibbutz Merhavia.

Yaakov Shabtai, or as his contemporaries referred to him, Yankale—one of Israel's important writers and playwrights, who died of a heart attack at the age of forty-seven—arrived in Merhavia for a Hashomer Hatzair youth camp in the summer of 1950, at the age of sixteen. It was then that he met Edna, who was half a year younger and the daughter of David Hanegbi, founder and editor of the Sifriat Hapoalim Publishing House. It was love at first sight. According to Edna, "a group of Hashomer Hatzair youngsters from Tel Aviv arrived for the summer camp. He didn't want to stay. They arrived on a Friday and he intended to leave for Tel Aviv on Sunday." That Friday evening everybody went to a teach-in of spirituals in the kibbutz dining hall. Edna was able to recall years afterward "the voice of that beautiful, curly-headed boy, full of joi-de-vivre, who sat behind her." She saw him again the next evening at the

---

74 Klein, interview.
75 Ibid.

folk dances. That's when they first introduced themselves. Edna was an excellent dancer. "We met that Saturday evening." He didn't leave and they started going out for long night walks. In her autobiographical novel Edna writes about a foursome—she paired with Yaakov; and her older friend Naomi, with her boyfriend, Barke.

Yaakov had just completed his sixth year of high school and had two more to go. From that summer on they were a couple. "We would go hitchhiking, meet up, write letters to each other," Edna recalled. When I asked for her impressions of Yaakov, Edna replied that "he was tall, good looking, open and happy. He was a good man. Not critical or judgmental." After graduating the Tikhon Hadash high school in Tel Aviv and completing his army service, Yaakov joined kibbutz Sasa in the Upper Galilee for a time. When he married Edna in the mid-fifties, he moved to Merhavia, where they lived for the next twelve years—unlike his younger brother, Aharon, who stayed in Merhavia as a youngster for just three years. In the summer of 1967, shortly after the Six Day War, the family moved to Tel Aviv.[76]

While in Merhavia, Yaakov gained a reputation as an excellent worker. He held various jobs there over the years: among others, he was in charge of a pig farm, worked in the fields, and taught at the kibbutz ulpan, a Hebrew school for new immigrants. He was also active in the cultural life of the kibbutz. Already as a teenager in Tel Aviv, he had written operetta-like texts that were performed at social functions of the Hashomer Hatzair's *ken merkaz*. One of Yaakov's earliest literary achievements was "The Game of Time," a musical staged in Merhavia in the summer of 1961, marking the fiftieth anniversary of the founding of the first Jewish settlement in the Valley. The musical juxtaposes the artificial and frenetic pace of urban existence with the nature-oriented and peaceful conditions of life on a kibbutz.[77]

When he died in Tel Aviv in early August 1981, an announcement was posted on the Merhavia dining room board: "Transportation to the funeral of Yaakov Shabtai of blessed memory will leave at 13:00 to the Holon Cemetery. Kibbutz members and friends who wish to make the trip should list their names." Among the twenty-seven signatures were those of Eytan Giladi, Hava Yasur, and Shalom Lurie.[78]

---

76 Edna Shabtai, interview by author, Tel Aviv, September 2009; Edna Shabtai, *For Love Is Strong as Death* [in Hebrew] (Jerusalem: Keter Publishers, 1986), 16–17.
77 *Haaretz*, October 3, 2014.
78 Yaakov Shabtai File, Merhavia Archive.

A journalist who visited Merhavia three years later spoke to a few of the people who had known Yaakov. A neighbor and friend, Dani Umanski, described him as a "walking volcano." The eighty-year-old Yaakov Tsamri recalled that "there was something attractive about him, a kind of magic. He was full of life. He loved people. He loved women." People remembered him as a superb storyteller. Even the most judgmental kibbutzniks were ready to look the other way, the few times when Yaakov wasn't working at his best. Everybody liked being in his company. His vitality and personal charm were overwhelming. People also, however, recalled moments of depression, referred to by Yaakov as "going down into the cellar" or "being in a fucked-up condition."

Having since moved to kibbutz Gan Shmuel, Ethan Giladi—Yaakov's close friend and his partner in the writing and production of "The Game of Time"—spoke of the void left in Merhavia once Yaakov returned to Tel Aviv. When asked why Yaakov never wrote about Merhavia, Giladi quoted Yaakov's own words: "He told me once that he would have liked to write about the kibbutz but he couldn't do it yet. He needed more time to pass. He didn't want to hurt people during their lifetime. He wasn't afraid of his own family, about whom he wrote so much in his books. He was scared of the kibbutz."[79]

Aharon Shabtai, Yaakov's younger brother, born in 1939, became an acclaimed poet and a noted translator of ancient Greek poetry and drama. He arrived in Merhavia in the mid-fifties when he was fifteen or sixteen. He lived and studied in the local boarding school from which he graduated in 1957. He was then drafted into the army and did not return to the kibbutz. His first poems were published in *Al Hamishmar* when he was still a high-school student in Merhavia.

Aharon's home in Merhavia was his peer-group's quarters. In a lengthy poem, "Kibbutz," published in the early 1970s, he describes objects and situations from everyday kibbutz life:

> In the boarding school
> Each grade
> Has its house
> Each house
> Six rooms
> Each room

---

[79] Yaara Zeira, "Expanses of Tel Aviv and the Confines of Merhavia," *Bemakhane Hanachal*, November 28, 1984.

> Four beds
> At one end of the corridor
> The classroom
> At the other
> Toilets and showers
> And the nurse's room.

He spoke of the communal dining hall and the kitchen:

> This building is called the *khadar okhel*
> It stands on a hill
> The Kibbutz is eating salad
> I stand near a small stainless steel table
> I love the machine for peeling potatoes
> And the bread-slicing machine
> I soak radishes in one sink
> And carrots in the other.

He goes on to describe a most demanding kind of work:

> And then we lifted four loads of hay
> Hay that had blackened in rain
> Some ropes have rotted
> We lift a bundle up onto the cart
> With two pitchforks.[80]

In an interview published ten years later, Aharon looked back and remarked that, "after the War of Independence there was an anticlimax of sorts, a revulsion with the spirit of Zionism and pioneering, and an ironic and sentimental perception of reality took hold instead. My view was that one should live inside reality and enjoy it."[81]

Aharon was popular with the girls, like his older brother. In his poem "Kibbutz," he remarked on the subject: "Our class met with another class that had arrived for a day's work on the kibbutz. And we discussed literature. And

---

80 Aharon Shabtai, *Kibbutz: Poems* [in Hebrew] (Tel Aviv: Hakibbutz Hameuchad Publishers, 1973).
81 Helit Yeshurun, *How Did You Do It? Interviews with Poets* [in Hebrew] (Tel Aviv: Hakibbutz Hameuchad Publishers, 2016), 264.

I fell in love with two or three girls from Beit Alfa." Already as an adolescent, Aharon Shabtai had his erotic preferences:

> My ideal
> Is a girl in panties
> Doing some housework
> With a hairy armpit
> Loveless life
> Stupid.[82]

It was during his Merhavia years that he began to write poetry. As he later remarked,

> When I arrived in kibbutz Merhavia to study at the boarding school I was introduced to Tuvia Ruebner, the literature teacher. His office was in Beit Zvi, on the second floor just under the tiled roof. After reading my poems he introduced me to Leah Goldberg. Those were the Leah Goldberg years: I would travel to Tel Aviv to hear her lecture at the Tzavta Center on Dizengoff street. In those years, when I was in the 11th and 12th grades, I used to send her my poems.[83]

Naomi and Barke were close friends of Yaakov Shabtai. Naomi was also friendly with Edna Negbi, Yankale's future wife; Barke had spent much of his Tel Aviv childhood at the Shabtais.

For years, the story of Naomi and Barke was the talk of the Hashomer Hatzair and its kibbutzim. Naomi got pregnant when she was a high-school student at the Merhavia boarding school. Barke was about to graduate from the Tikhon Khadash high school in Tel Aviv. Naomi gave birth to twins on her nineteenth birthday. I asked her how the pregnancy affected her life. "I was immediately taken out of the boarding school and sent to live with my parents. They also put me onto the *siddur avoda*—the work-assignment list. Nobody really discussed my new situation with me."[84]

---

82 Shabtai, *Kibbutz*.
83 Aharon Shabtai, *Yediot Aharonot*, July 2009.
84 Naomi and Barke Harpaz, interview by author, Tel Aviv, December 2014.

I remember Naomi as the sexiest girl in the boarding school. I saw her on various occasions during my stay in the kibbutz, but only spoke to her recently. I was familiar with the story of the twins and eager to learn what her sex life had been like during a period when I could only dream about it. Both Naomi and Barke recalled that the attitude toward sex was rather puritan in all the kibbutzim of Hashomer Hatzair.

Naomi's parents arrived in Palestine from Poland in 1929 and joined Merhavia three years later. Naomi was born there in 1933. Her peer group, Shalhevet, consisted of more outside children than native ones; a few of the former were Holocaust survivors. That balance wasn't an easy one for the locals, according to Naomi. Barke's family lived in Tel Aviv, in the same neighborhood as the Shabtai brothers' family, and he was a close friend of Yaakov from the age of three. Barke clearly recalls that Merhavia summer camp of 1950, when he first met Naomi and when Yaakov paired off with Edna: "My school and its legendary principal Tony accepted my new status as father much better than the progressive socialists of Merhavia accepted Naomi's." The wedding was in the Tel Aviv apartment of Barke's parents. Tony attended. The only ones to arrive from Merhavia were Naomi's family. In Merhavia, according to Naomi, there was a lot of gossip. She recalls that period as "the dark days." Still, Naomi and Barke lived in the kibbutz for more than twenty years.[85]

Michal Bat Adam, who would later become a leading Israeli filmmaker, was an outside child—a *yaldat khutz*—in Merhavia for more than ten years. Her father, Adam Rubin, arrived in Palestine on the eve of the Second World War. Among his close friends in the Warsaw branch of Hashomer Hatzair were the future writer Binyamin Tenenbaum (Tene) and the future sculptor Natan Rapoport, who would create the world-famous monument of the Warsaw ghetto fighters. Adam became an artist-photographer. Michal's mother, Yemima, though she came from a religious family, joined Hashomer Hatzair and met Adam at the Warsaw branch. Yemima arrived in Palestine before Adam. Michal recalls that her parents used to speak Polish when she was a child, and that Polish was actually her first language. The family lived for a short while in Kiryat Haim and in Haifa, finally settling in Afula. That's where they raised their girls, Neta and Michal. Adam opened a photo shop in the center of town and became

---

85 Ibid.

well known throughout the Valley. Yemima mostly remained at home but was barely able to take care of her daughters. She suffered from attacks of manic-depression and needed to be hospitalized from time to time. Adam, torn between family and work, decided to place the girls in a kibbutz. It was only natural that the kibbutz would be Merhavia, very near to Afula, where the family was living at the time. The first to leave home was Neta, the older sister. She joined the Shibolet group in the boarding school. The six-year-old Michal joined the Zamir group in the summer of 1951. That's just when I left Gefen and the kibbutz. Her time in Merhavia as a young girl and as a teenager have been vividly depicted in her autobiographical films and in her memoir.[86]

Michal recalls her craving for music and her first love. Both were connected with Merhavia. She remembers her deep disappointment when she wasn't allowed to study the piano and had to study the violin instead: "It's a Saturday afternoon. Father and mother came to visit me in the kibbutz and we are on our way to the music teacher's room. The music teacher lives in a stone house with an arched front. This is one of the earliest houses in the kibbutz." Although no real names are mentioned in her films and in her book, I immediately recognized the music teacher as Galila, Tuvia Ruebner's wife. Their room was located in one of the oldest structures, in the central yard of the kibbutz. The music teacher was quite nice to Michal, but wouldn't give in to her pleas. Michal had a strong feeling that it had to do with her being an "outsider."[87]

One of the opening sequences in Michal's film *Boy Takes Girl* portrays the collective shower and the mixed living quarters. These illustrate the closeness and togetherness of the peer group. According to Michal Bat Adam, "the *kvutza*, the group, is your family. It's everything." Collective showering ended when they were in the sixth grade, but sleeping in the same room with boys continued until graduation. It wasn't easy for her. Members of the peer group weren't entirely of an equal status. In the case of her particular group, it was mainly talent that increased the status of a boy or a girl. Almost half of the kids in her group played various musical instruments.

As for her feelings and emotions as a yaldat khutz, Michal distinctly recalls that upon arrival in Merhavia she was given only part of the kibbutz clothing, so that for some time she had to wear a blouse that she'd brought with her,

---

86 Michal Bat Adam, interview by author, Tel Aviv, March 2015; Boy Takes Girl: film, 1982; Aya: An Imagined Autobiography, film, 1994; Michal Bat Adam, *An Imagined Autobiography* [in Hebrew] (Tel Aviv: Yediot Aharonot Publishers, 2002); Doron Halutz, "Just a Human Being," *Haaretz* (May 14, 2010): 50–56.
87 Bat Adam, *An Imagined Autobiography*, 44–45.

which was different from those worn by the other girls in her group. This made her feel even more of an outcast. On another occasion, she voluntarily handed over something she was wearing out of a sense of inferiority toward the other girls. And although in time she became part of the group, her self-identity as a yaldat khutz never left her: "the feeling of being a *yaldat khutz* is for life." When I asked her about in-group relations and nicknaming, she declined to mention any specifics but remembered that there was a girl in her group who "would become completely devastated when somebody called her that name. There was also one boy whom the group really tormented."

Music was a most significant aspect of Michal's life in Merhavia. "It was something to hold on to, it replaced my absent parents," she claimed. Besides playing the violin she also joined the choir, and when passed over for a solo role was deeply disappointed: "Such things could devastate me, I was more sensitive than the others. I didn't have my parents nearby." Michal and her sister were adopted by the Reich family. The mother, Khancia, was the kibbutz shoemaker. When I asked Michal whether the family showed her any signs of affection, she replied that "they were very-matter-of-fact people. They didn't hug their own children and of course they didn't hug me either."[88]

I was curious to learn about gender and sexuality in Michal's life, starting from her early years in the Merhavia grade school and up to her adolescence in the boarding school. Her film *Boy Takes Girl* has a quite dramatic scene in which two of the kibbutz boys convince the protagonist to play doctor and patient with them. "The minute I lie down on the bed they attack me like two birds of prey. They take off my panties and start to press and knead me in a very painful way. I yell, but they don't let up. As if I don't exist," the protagonist narrates. A similar event takes place a few years later: "Somebody in the trees calls out my name. I see that it's David the redhead. I try to walk away but he doesn't let me pass." A short exchange between the two ensues, as the heroine reports: "'Let me go.' '—Only if you let me embrace you.' David grabs me strongly. His hand is under my shirt. He kneads my breasts. I try to free myself. I kick him and yell. He covers my mouth with his. It hurts and I can't breathe. He has a terrible smell. I wish he would die."[89]

In her film and in her memoir, she also relives her first sexual attraction and first love, at the age of fifteen or sixteen. Love and music were always linked in Michal's Merhavia years. She was very much attracted to her violin teacher.

---

88 Bat Adam, interview.
89 *Boy Takes Girl*; Bat Adam, *An Imagined Autobiography*, 60–61, 70–71.

A sequence shows her walking into his room in the middle of the night. They sit together on his bed. "He strokes my hair. 'Tell me what's going on.' 'I've nothing to say.' He puts his hand on my shoulder and we are close to each other. This is bliss." The scene ends, however, with the man leading her to the door and persuading her to return to her quarters.[90]

Her first love was apparently "Hagai," a boy two years older than her who studied the piano. She tried to get his attention in a very subtle way: "He smiled and I noticed that his head is getting closer to mine and when we were really close I was so mixed up that I don't recall how it all started. I just remember him in my mouth, his lips and mine, and my face burning." It was in the late evening of that day that they made love for the first time. "First we decided to go to the orange-grove, then to the railway tracks, finally we went to the eucalyptus trees. The darkness and the wind brought us very close to each other. Hagai unbuttoned my shirt, looked at me in the moonlight and said that I'm so beautiful that this must be a dream, that it couldn't be real, that he is so happy. He suggested that we go someplace and both of us thought simultaneously of the shed where I'd been practicing my music."[91] After leaving Merhavia to help out at home in Haifa, Michal used to come back to visit her sister who remained there for good. She never really spoke with her previous peer-group members. "It was just hello and good-by."

Finally I asked Michal to what extent those years in Merhavia shaped her opinions and attitudes in later life. "Hashomer Hatzair and Merhavia instilled in me a kind of extreme honesty, a sense of justice, contentment," she replied. According to Michal, there was always a certain duality in the very essence of life in Merhavia: "On the one hand there was open-mindedness in matters of spirit such as literature and music. At the same time, personal relations in Merhavia made me think metaphorically of soil that's been tamped down and has never been aired."[92]

I was, of course, most eager to talk to members of my own group, now in their seventies. Yoel Mintzer was the only member of Gefen who had reacted to my criticism of Merhavia in the *Al Hamishmar* interview. He showed both

---

90   Bat Adam, *An Imagined Autobiography*, 75–77.
91   Ibid., 84–85.
92   Bat Adam, interview.

understanding and empathy. He and his wife, Ruthi, hosted me in their house when I visited the kibbutz many years afterward.

Yoel's parents were among the founders of Merhavia. His father was from Drohobycz; his mother, from Lviv. They never spoke with him about the old country. His uncle Yosef mentioned it only once.[93] In a succinct remark, Yoel summed up what apparently applied to much of his generation: "It seems that we the [kibbutz] children, were meant to be 'the New Man': a man that does not speak Yiddish, isn't concerned with his parents' past, has to be 'Spartan' and prefers ideology over emotion. In a sense we were crippled. We were told that what is important is the collective, never the individual."[94]

Since I am quite fascinated with the question of sexuality in Gefen, this was one of the first subjects I raised with Yoel. "Intimate relations between adolescents was a forbidden topic in the movement," he told me. When I inquired about his personal experiences, he spoke about his girlfriend who was with us in Gefen: beautiful Abigail. "We used to walk in the vineyard, just behind the 'Gefen' house. We would lie there in the dark and embrace. I would touch her belly. Anything above or below was forbidden stuff. These restraints remained internalized even later on. There was no sexual openness whatsoever." Yoel's response to my intimate personal questions was exceptionally sincere. When I asked him about his memory of mixed showers he told me, "I suffered more than once from erections upon entering the shower. The theory of sublimation didn't work in my case." He also spoke about peer pressure from the group. "There was a lot of collective criticism and self-criticism. Many tears were shed during group discussions."[95]

I also asked Yoel for his overall opinion of Merhavia. He spoke about the social and psychological features of his kibbutz. Unlike Mishmar Haemek, the founding members of which had mostly come from large Polish cities like Warsaw and Lodz, Merhavia in its first years consisted of young people from small Galician towns. A small-town mentality persisted in their new lives, too. There was a feeling of closeness and intimacy in a rather negative sense: "Each one stuck his nose in the other fellow's butt." Although additional groups joined Merhavia over the years, "the initial organizational and social culture of the old timers has always prevailed." Some of the old-timers were quite arrogant. Janek Shutzberg was one of them. "He could never shut up and listen to the other guy," Yoel said.

---

93 Yoel Mintzer, letter to author, May 17, 2009; Yoel Mintzer, interview by author, July 2009.
94 Mintzer, interview.
95 Ibid.

There were, however, a few old-timers that Yoel liked and adored. One of them was Itsio Rand, who was in charge of the kibbutz carpentry shop. They worked together for twenty-five years." I really loved him. He started his carpentry apprenticeship at the age of fifteen as a youngster in Galicia, and continued as a carpenter in Merhavia up to the age of eighty-five. He was a good man and a giving person."[96]

Yoel recalled the first death in Gefen. It was Ehud, a paratrooper, killed in the Gaza action of 1955. This had happened a few years after I left Merhavia, but the sad news reached me somehow. According to Yoel, "this was a shock for all of us. I recall his funeral in the kibbutz cemetery. His parents, Aliza and Artek turned his room into a kind of sanctuary and nearly forced us to come and visit them whenever we were on leave from the army."[97]

We spoke about relations within the kvutza, the peer group, and about various boys and girls. Toward the end of the interview, I asked him how he regarded the Gefen group now, after all these years. Yoel, to my surprise, was very proud of Gefen. It was, according to him, the only peer group in the Merhavia boarding school that kept on meeting annually for decades. I myself participated recently in one such get-together. When I asked him about their feelings of superiority and inability to accept youngsters who were not Merhavia-born sabras, Yoel remarked, "we should be able to forgive and look back with compassion."

I hadn't seen Ezra and Esther for almost sixty years. When I met them, both were open and friendly. Ezra was among the very few Gefen boys whom I remembered fondly. I spent many hours in their house reminiscing and discussing Gefen and Merhavia.[98]

Ezra's parents, Yaakov and Tsivia, were born in eastern Galicia, when it was still part of the Hapsburg Empire. His father's family lived in Sambor, and his mother's, in nearby Turka. Both were among the founders of Merhavia. His father held various manual jobs in the kibbutz but was most known as an outstanding baker. He served as kibbutz secretary, as well. Ezra's mother was among the first educators in the Kibbutz Haartzi movement. I asked

---
96 Ibid.
97 Ibid.
98 Tsamri, interview.

Ezra about his childhood memories concerning relations with his parents. "It was rather warm, but there wasn't much of physical touch." He did remember Hadassah, his kindergarten teacher. "She was wonderful. She instilled in me the feeling for creativity. Once she woke us up to see the morning star." In time, Ezra started to draw and paint. I was interested in his memories of the boarding high school. "We went down to the boarding school in the fifth grade, in 1946. We were ten at that time." The Gefen group joined Hashomer Hatzair two years later. Ezra recalled it as a significant moment in his life. "There was an impressive celebration. We got green scarfs and blue shirts with white laces." In time, Ezra became a madrich, a counselor, of a younger group. "The highest point of my activity in the youth movement was when I was chosen to head the Merhavia ken, branch, of Hashomer Hatzair." Ezra recalled heated political discussions between his parents. "Father's ideas were close to those of Mapai, while mother was more to the left and supported Mapam. The family nearly broke up. Father used to criticize Meir Yaari. Once he even shouted at him, 'we should not parrot the Soviet Union!' All this happened in the early 1950s."

I was most interested to hear Ezra's memories of the relations between the Merhavia-born youngsters in the Gefen group and the yaldei khutz—the outside children. "I know that our attitude toward the outsiders wasn't positive. I do recall that the attitude towards you wasn't good. We used to tease you. I have no idea why. Perhaps we never liked those who were different. We called you skirki. Aza, a yaldat khutz, was nicknamed kusa (pussy). There was something quite sadistic in our behavior."

I was eager to hear how his relations with Esther, his future wife, had started, when they were fourteen or fifteen. Esther was one of the girls who survived the Holocaust in Poland and joined Gefen in 1946. "Esther's foster parents in the kibbutz were Khanka and Yaakov Reich, my parents' neighbors. I would see Esther every day rinsing tea glasses outside the house, dressed in those short hot pants. That's when she attracted me for the first time. I recall that when we became a couple and our group went on hikes, I always tried to sleep near her." I asked Ezra whether Esther spoke about her childhood in Poland. "She never spoke about it. She started talking about it after years, when we were already married and had children, when she returned to Poland for the first time." Toward the end of the interview, I asked Ezra about his thoughts and feelings concerning the changes in the essence of the kibbutz. "It was very difficult for me to accept these changes. I loved the kibbutz as it used to be. I miss it to this very day."

The next day I interviewed Esther. She was ten when she arrived in Merhavia, in April 1946. "We stayed in a transit camp, in Atlit. From there we were taken to a house on the Carmel, in Haifa. Tsilka Man, from Merhavia, took us from there to the kibbutz. A crowd was waiting on the lawn, near the dining hall. They surrounded us on all sides. And then they took us straight to the boarding school, to the Gefen house."

Esther was born in Ciechanowiec, southwest of Bialystok, in 1935. She had three brothers: Gershon, Itshe, and Arie. She was the youngest. They spoke Yiddish at home, so little Esther hardly knew Polish. The family was well off, and Esther nursed happy, though foggy and fragmentary, memories of her childhood. "I recall distinctly those gorgeous yellow sunflowers in the garden near our house." She remembered the looks and smells of her mother's cooking and baking: "the borsht, the kneydlach, the sweet leykach, the honey cake." Esther's father was deported by the Soviets and died in Russia during the war. Prior to the war, he was in the timber business, so the family had friendly relations with a number of households in nearby villages. It was the Bialys who sheltered them for three years. "These people assisted us in times of distress. This, of course, involved considerable danger for them and their family." Esther's oldest brother, Gershon, was killed when he tried to join the partisans. Esther's mother and her brother Itshe were shot by neighbors. Only Esther and Arie survived.[99]

Esther had quite pleasant memories of her arrival in Merhavia. She arrived there with three other girls, child survivors from Poland. "Many wanted to be our foster families. My foster parents were the Reichs. The mother, Khantsia, was the kibbutz shoemaker. Her daughter Naomi was somewhat older than me and we became friends. David Meisler, who was later killed during the War of Independence, was an excellent teacher. He took good care of us." Esther was also lucky that she had her older brother in kibbutz Gan-Shmuel, not too far from Merhavia. When I asked her about her memories of wartime, she was sure that she was always aware of it, but "nobody asked and nobody spoke about it." It was during the War of Independence that her traumatic past from wartime Poland surfaced dramatically. "Suddenly there was shooting again. There were airplanes and bombs."

As for everyday life within her Gefen peer group, Esther did not recall any specific difficulties, except for the collective showers. "We did not understand how boys and girls could shower together and swim nude in the kibbutz pool." For a while, the new girls showered separately. "In a month or two we decided to take showers with the others."

---

99 Esther Tsamri, interview by author, Merhavia, May 12, 2009; Esther Tsamri, *Childhood with Straw and Pigs* (Jerusalem: Yad Sara, 2010).

When Esther met with her brother they used to speak Yiddish. In time, they started speaking Hebrew to each other. They often recalled their family. "Still, I continued to miss my family, especially my mother. Sometimes I would cry softly at night." Esther continued to converse in Yiddish with her distant relatives in Haifa. Yiddish stayed with her, actually, throughout her life.

Esther's first postwar visit to Poland and to her native town was in October 1987. She and her brother joined one of the first tourist groups from Israel, since individual travel to Poland was still impossible at that time. When they arrived at their prewar house, Esther was overwhelmed. "I just sat there and cried." She traveled to Poland again in 1994, that time with Ezra, her brother, and her brother's wife. The third time, in 2007, Esther was accompanied by her adult children. Her next "Polish project" was to take her grandchildren to her hometown and to the village where she was saved. Esther's Polish saviors were awarded the Righteous Gentiles medal in 2002. Esther started sharing her wartime and Holocaust memories not only with her own family but with a wider public as well. "I tell my story every year in my grandchildren's classes on the Holocaust Day." One of the high points of Esther's return to the past was the lighting of a torch at Yad Vashem, at the public Holocaust Day ceremony in 2005. She insisted that her oldest grandson, Amitai, light the torch with her.

Gideon Weiss was my closest friend in Gefen. For a long time I made efforts to locate him, without success. It was only in 2009 that we met again. Since he had been an outsider, a yeled khutz somewhat like myself, I was eager to hear his impressions and memories of Merhavia and of our peers.

Gideon arrived in Merhavia from Haifa in the mid-1940s, when he was nine or ten years old. His mother had died and his father had remarried. When a new baby was born to his parents, Gideon was sent to the kibbutz. His father had been close to the Mapam party and knew people in Merhavia. Gideon, unexpectedly for me, recalled his years there as a very happy time: "I didn't miss home at all. I adapted very fast. My foster parents were the Cnaanis. This was a very warm family, excellent people." As for Gefen, Gideon's recollections were mostly good ones. His relations with the girls were like those of the Merhavia-born boys. There was no sexual attraction. He felt like a sibling.

Still, he admitted that the kibbutz-born youngsters "were more secure, felt like the owners of the place." Like myself, Gideon left Merhavia in the summer of 1951. His father insisted that he continue his schooling in a vocational school in Haifa. When I asked whether he later kept in contact at all with Merhavia, his answer was unequivocal: "This was a complete break. It angered them. To leave the kibbutz in those days was high treason."[100]

Figure 2.1 The founders of kibbutz Merhavia. *Second row from top:* Meir Yaari, first from right; Shaya Nir, fourth from left. Woman in dotted dress, Pnina Nir nee Bomze. *Second row from bottom:* Tuvia Yaari, first from left. Courtesy Merhavia Archive.

Figure 2.2 In front of the "Gefen" house: Esther, Michael Oppenheimer, and the author.

---

100 Gideon Weiss, interview by author, Tel Aviv, February 2009.

Figure 2.3 Merhavia's Great Courtyard, 1917. Courtesy of Hakibbutz Hameuchad Publishing House Ltd.

Kibbutz Merhavia • CHAPTER 2 | 63

Figure 2.4 The author, posing on the new "Ferguson" tractor.

Figure 2.5 "From sea to sea" march. *First row from bottom*: Gideon Weiss, first from left. *Upper row*: Bela, second from left; Esther, fifth from left; *Far right, on top*: the author, wearing hat.

Figure 2.6 Camping out. Abigail and Ezra.

Figure 2.7 The "Gefen" group. *Bottom row,*: Ehud. fourth from left. *Second row*: Yoel, third from left; Bela, sixth from left. *Standing on the far right*: Ezra. *Top left corner*: Esther.

Figure 2.8 Ehud in paratrooper's uniform.

CHAPTER 3

Afula

When I left Merhavia, I went to live with my mother in the nearby town of Afula, a twenty-minutes' walk from the kibbutz. Afula, the unofficial "capital" of the Valley, has been often ridiculed for its hopes to be a major metropolis. It has ended up as one of the most provincial towns in Israel.

Afula is situated in Jezreel Valley, an ancient crossroads and one of the earliest locations for the modern Jewish settlement in Palestine. The Valley is the site of some of the oldest kibbutzim in the country, including Ein Harod, Beit Hashita, Beit Alfa, Mishmar Haemek, and Merhavia. Of the total of twenty kibbutzim established in Mandatory Palestine in the 1920s, fourteen are in the Valley. Some of these kibbutzim, like Ein Harod and Merhavia, were much more than communal agricultural settlements. They constituted the political and cultural backbones of their respective kibbutz movements. Some of the most prominent leaders of the Jewish Yishuv and the early State of Israel lived there: Yitzhak Tabenkin in Ein Harod, Meir Yaari in Merhavia, Yaakov Hazan in Mishmar Haemek. In addition to the kibbutzim, some of the oldest Jewish *moshavim*, cooperative villages—including Nahalal, Kfar Yehoshua, Tel Adashim, and Balfouria—were also located in the Valley. A disproportionately high percentage of the political leadership in the first years of the state came from the Valley. Of the 120 members of the first Knesset, the Israeli parliament, sixteen were Valley residents. These included Tabenkin and Zizling in Ein Harod, Yaari in Merhavia, Hazan in Mishmar Haemek, and Shmuel Dayan in Nahalal.[1]

Ha'emek, the Valley, has been a prominent theme of much of Israeli prose, poetry, and songs. Yitzhak Dov Berkowitz and Shmuel Yosef Agnon, who visited the kibbutzim in the Valley, presented a somewhat naïve and idealistic image of kibbutz life. The younger writers and poets who actually lived on those kibbutzim were more realistic and critical. Among the latter were such

---

1 Mordehai Naor, "Jezreel Valley—The Cradle of the Kibbutzim," in *Jezreel Valley, 1900–1967* [in Hebrew], ed. Mordehai Naor (Jerusalem: Ben Zvi Institute Publishers, 1993), 54–71.

poets as Natan Yonatan in kibbutz Sarid and Ayin Hillel in kibbutz Mishmar Haemek. A young writer whose early prose is full of depictions of the actual conditions of kibbutz life in the Valley was Moshe Shamir, a member of Mishmar Haemek in the 1940s. Another writer whose novels depict kibbutz life, especially kibbutz youth, is Reuven Kritz, whom I visited and interviewed a few years ago in Düsseldorf. Born in Germany, Kritz arrived at kibbutz Mizra, a few minutes' drive from Afula, in 1938. He later went to study and live in Mishmar Haemek's boarding school. Eli Amir, who arrived from Iraq, describes his first years in early Israel in his widely acclaimed autobiographical novel *Scapegoat*. In those years, he was a member of an immigrant youth group in Mishmar Haemek. His novel is extremely critical of the kibbutz community and its patronizing attitudes toward new immigrants, especially oriental Jews.[2]

What has been the image of the Valley in Israeli Zionist culture? According to the popular Israeli songwriter Yoram Tharlev, "the Valley was the most conspicuous symbol of the realization of the Zionist dream." Some of the most beloved songs of "good old Eretz Israel" were in fact about the Valley. According to Ariel Hirszfeld, the Valley was not only a real, tangible space, but also a spiritual space—and, in a way, even a quasi-religious one—for those who settled there and for those who wrote about it. The local poetry and the Valley songs spoke of its specific landscapes and of the fusion between its nature and its people. "[These] Valley songs were infused with specific music."[3]

The Jezreel Valley region surrounding the future town of Afula was owned in the late nineteenth century by a wealthy Arab family from Beirut. The town's site at the time was an Ottoman estate with just a few stone houses. Its Arab name was Fula. The Turkish authorities built a railway station there in 1905. The station became one of the stops on the Haifa-to-Syria route. Jewish settlers would refer to the train as *Rakevet Haemek*: Valley Railway. The beginnings of Jewish Afula date from the wave of immigration of the mid-1920s, consisting mainly of Polish middle-class Jews. It was at that time that a US-based land development company by the name of Kehilat Zion purchased lands in the area and began making plans for a modern Jewish city, similar to Tel Aviv, which would serve as an urban center for the surrounding agricultural settlements. The German-Jewish architect Richard Kaufman, the planner of Nahalal,

---

2 Avner Holzman, "Jezreel Valley in Hebrew Literature," in *Jezreel Valley*, 216–21, 223–24.
3 Nathan Shahar et al., eds., *Songs and Poems from the Israeli Valley* [in Hebrew] (Bnei Brak: Hakibbutz Hameuchad Publishers, 2005), 8–9, 88–93.

was asked to design the new city. The first Jewish settlers of modern Afula to purchase land and begin construction of residential and commercial structures arrived in the winter of 1925. One of them, who would later own an impressive garments store in the center of town, recalled that "taking a real shower at the end of a working day was a wishful dream. A couple of mules harnessed to a carriage with a black barrel used to bring us water from Merhavia." Several groups of pioneers that were living communally set up and moved into shacks and tents as they built the town. Some of these communes were affiliated with Hashomer Hatzair. Dozens of unaffiliated laborers arrived as well. Close to a hundred families and a few hundred laborers constituted the nucleus of the future town.[4]

Afula seemed like a dynamic and promising economic and human enterprise. The first half of 1926 saw a further increase in housing and population. An official report submitted in the summer of 1926 told of 218 families, 59 buildings, and 155 shacks. The overall number of inhabitants, including several hundred laborers, reached 1,600. A boulevard of palm trees, which would become a town landmark, was planted in the center. However, everyday realities and a severe economic crisis soon shattered these plans and hopes. Many construction projects were discontinued and the population fell. The number of laborers declined by a half. Some of the initial middle-class settlers departed. It wasn't until the mid-1930s that things began to pick up again. A moderate number of new settlers arrived in Afula. The permanent population of the town now exceeded a thousand. New buildings went up. One of them was the Great Synagogue at the southern entrance to the town. Another, one of the most impressive structures built in Afula in the late 1930s, was the Tegart police fort, in the center of town. Throughout the 1940s, there was slow and steady progress. New businesses were established. A planned neighborhood in the north of town, along the road to Valley Hospital, went up in the mid-forties. By 1950, over eighty houses in it were populated. A school for local children opened there around that time. When the neighborhood project was completed, it had more than a hundred one-story houses, each with its own garden. This was *Shkhunat Hapoalim*—the Workers' Quarter. Notwithstanding its unprepossessing name, in time it became a quite comfortable, green, middle-class neighborhood. My uncle Zeev's house was part of that neighborhood.[5]

---

4 Dan Giladi, "Afula: The Valley Town or a Town Facing the Valley," in *Jezreel Valley*, 97–100.
5 Giladi, "Afula," 104.

As for Afula itself, what finally emerged from the initial plan of a big city with an opera house, was a rather small provincial town. The surrounding kibbutzim seemed to be self-sufficient in terms of services, and they looked down on the nearby shabby, diaspora-type middle-class town from the vantage point of their pioneering communal lifestyle. Many of the agricultural settlers in the Valley as well as people from other parts of the country viewed Afula as no more than a transit point and bus depot en route to various destinations. By 1950, about one hundred bus lines had stations in the Afula Egged bus depot, located in the center of town.[6]

Afula was never on the front lines of the War of Independence, though it was shelled several times. The most dramatic event occurred on a Friday evening, in early June 1948. A shell hit two houses, killing five people. Nineteen young men from Afula also perished in various battles throughout the country.[7]

The real boost to Afula came only in the early 1950s, following mass immigration. Eastern European—mainly Romanian—Jews and Jews from Arab countries, mainly Iraq and Yemen, settled there. From two thousand inhabitants in 1948, the population of Afula grew to three thousand in 1949, then to six thousand in 1950; it passed the ten thousand mark in 1954. Three huge maabarot, transit facilities for the newcomers, were erected inside and near the town. New public buildings were built. One of them was Kolron Cinema, which at times also housed theatrical and musical performances. My years in Afula coincided with that period.[8]

At least two sites located a few kilometers outside of town were in a sense considered part of Afula: Valley Hospital and *Kfar Yeladim*, or the Children's Village. The hospital's beginnings in the 1920s were very modest. Its first permanent buildings opened to service the town's and the Valley's population in 1930. The hospital had a staff of fewer than forty at that time. That number increased to sixty in 1940, was close to a hundred in 1945, was 154 in 1950, and 274 in 1955. One of the best wards was the children's ward, under the direction of Professor Erich Nassau. Unlike most other wards, which mainly accepted patients from Valley settlements, that ward drew sick children from all over Palestine—and later, Israel—for examinations and hospitalization. The

---

6 Ibid., 95–112; *The City of Jezreel—Afula, 1925–1950* [in Hebrew] (Afula: Afula Local Council, 1950), 118.
7 *The City of Jezreel*, 103.
8 Zeev Vilnai, *Afula: Jezreel Town* [in Hebrew] (Afula: Afula Local Council, 1966), passim.

most prominent pediatricians besides Dr. Nassau were Dr. Hanka Heruti and Dr. Yaakov Rotem.[9]

Kfar Yeladim—the Children's Village—located north of the hospital, was founded in the wake of the First World War and of the pogroms in Ukraine. It initially housed Jewish orphans. Soon, however, most of the orphans were found by their Jewish relatives already living in Palestine and were taken to live with them. New settlers arrived in the early 1920s but didn't remain there for long. Subsequently, the village buildings functioned in the 1940s as a facility for glider operations and then as a school for children from Afula and nearby settlements. Ultimately, it became a military base.

The school system in Afula consisted of two educational facilities: the religious Mizrahi School, at the southern edge of town; and the Labor Movement School, located first in Children's Village and, ultimately, in Afula's Workers' Quarter. Primary-school pupils and, later on, high-school students in that school came both from Afula proper and from nearby moshavim—workers' villages—including Balfouria and Tel Adashim. By 1950, the school had primary and high-school grades, with a total of 430 students.[10]

After living for a year and a half with my peers in Merhavia, I moved into a small and modest immigrant flat on the outskirts of Afula. There, I joined my mother, who until then had been living with uncle Zeev and aunt Pepka in their Workers' Quarter house. Of our two tiny rooms, one was rented out to strangers. At one time, our tenant was a single man with a limp, apparently a teacher. Then for a while, there were two female nurses, one Yemenite and the other Romanian. My mother worked at times as a cleaning lady. Only much later did I realize that all these arrangements were meant to enable me to study full time in the local high school and, eventually, to get my matriculation certificate. I tutored younger kids from time to time. My Romanian friend Nelu told me once we could earn some money reaping corn in a nearby field, so we did. I also worked for a while in the local office of the Histadrut clinic. One summer vacation, I had a job as a switchboard operator in Valley Hospital. During another vacation, I did secretarial work at the hospital's pathology department. In time,

---

9 Ibid.
10 *The City of Jezreel*, 112–13.

we began receiving some remuneration payments from Germany as Holocaust survivors. This improved our meager finances considerably.

My closest friend in Afula was Nelu. We studied in the same class and spent many hours together after school. His father ran a small hardware store on Palms' Boulevard. His family rented a small apartment in an old building, in the center of town. On Friday evenings, I would usually drop by, chat with his parents, and leave with Nelu to walk around town. We would stroll up and down Palms' Boulevard. On occasion, we would meet boys and girls from our school and hang out with them. Mostly we would just walk and talk. Nelu introduced me to an amateur theater group, a short while after my arrival in Afula. The organizer was a new immigrant from Romania who worked in the local post office. One of its members was Budiaga ("Bodo"), who would in time become a highly popular Israeli actor and comedian, performing mostly in Yiddish. When I called him up recently, he told me that whenever he is on stage in Afula, he tells the audience that that's where his acting career began. Our group had a few rehearsals and we finally premiered in the newly opened Kolron cinema hall. The play was about a group of Israeli soldiers in the War of Independence. I had been "wounded" and was carried on stage on a stretcher. Our Hebrew must have been quite poor, since we pronounced the nickname of one of the protagonists, Loksh—tall and thin in Hebrew slang—as "Lukash." Still, I enjoyed it a lot.

I managed to meet only one of my former teachers from Afula. Decades after my time there, I bumped into David Kochavi, completely by chance, at a reception at Haifa University. I recognized him immediately. He had barely changed. Still slim and sporting a mustache, I could imagine him just as he had been: standing in front of our class, leaning back on one leg. At Yad Vashem, I sat in meetings with Professor Arik Kochavi, a scholar of Nazi Germany and the Holocaust from Haifa University. I never associated him with my former high-school teacher of English literature from Afula—his father.

I interviewed David in his spacious high-rise apartment overlooking the Haifa port. I had a vague notion of his multicultural background, but it was only now that I learned the details of his unusual life story.

David was born in 1928 in Rovno, Volhynia, in the northeast of interwar Poland, and he grew up as a boy in nearby Rokitno. "My father worked as a photographer for the Polish Army and was a real Polish patriot. I recall Polish officers and soldiers whom I saw very often in our house. My dream was to become a soldier in the Polish Army."[11] David's father died when David was ten, and the family emigrated to Brazil. They settled in Natal. Young David, who spoke both Yiddish and Polish, now had to acquire a new language: Portuguese. "The only subjects that truly engaged my interest were the study of languages," he later claimed.[12] Over the next few years, David gained the ability to read Spanish, Russian, and German. A US Air Force base was established near the city during the war, and David, although still a teenager and a high-school student, acquired sufficient knowledge of English to work as an interpreter both in the city and on the base. The locals started referring to him as the "boy who speaks many languages."[13] Once he bumped into some Polish RAF pilots on the base, and he even considered joining the Polish Air Force in Britain. He was sixteen at the time, and his family was decisively against this adventure. It was on the US base that David met a Jewish military chaplain, Rabbi Baum, who suggested that he continue his education at Yeshiva University in New York. When David arrived in New York in the summer of 1945, he was seventeen. Although being a student of Jewish studies meant being on track to become a rabbi, young David led his life in three different worlds: Jewish, Polish, and Brazilian. He would soon become an ardent Zionist as well.[14]

It was in New York, with its enormous Jewish community, that young David fully grasped what had happened to European Jewry during the war. The Holocaust would have an enormous effect on his feelings, thoughts, and actions. David soon became an active member of the rightist Zionist Betar movement. He decided to forsake his rabbinical studies and to join the struggle for Jewish independence in Palestine.

He joined the crew of the *Exodus* in the United States and sailed with it to France in late February 1947. Although he was one of the crew and became friendly with the young Hebrew-speaking Haganah people running the operation, he unexpectedly found himself identifying instead with the Holocaust survivors once they boarded the ship: "Suddenly, I was one of the DP's climbing aboard. I spoke to them in Yiddish. I even addressed some in Polish. I was one of them." Quite soon, he came across Jews from his native town and was told in detail about the tragedy of the Jewish community and of

---

11 David Kochavi, interview by author, Haifa, September 2010; David Kochavi (Starec), *Tears among the Waves: From Exodus to Jerusalem* (New York: Epoch Publishing, 2008), 10.
12 Kochavi, *Tears among the Waves*, 48.
13 Ibid., 54.
14 Ibid., 77.

his family there. When the British commandeered the *Exodus* as it approached the port of Haifa in mid-July 1947, David was wounded, and a photo of him with a bandaged head soon became one of the iconic images of the Zionist struggle for aliyah. "Despite the excruciating pain in my head, I went out onto the deck. Many of the displaced persons—DPs—were standing there singing Hatikvah." Eventually, David ended up on one of the British boats that sailed back to Europe with illegal immigrants on board. During his stay in DP camps in Germany, he had some unpleasant encounters with Germans. Still, he didn't lose his faith in men: "even then, in Germany, in 1947, I forced myself to continue believing in the brotherhood of mankind." When he finally ended up in a DP camp in Marseilles, David went yet through another identity shift: "I was already trying hard to identify myself as a Palestinian Jew. I had already decided to join the Palmach."[15]

David was an idealist: quite naïve and quick to identify with people and causes that affected him at different points in his life. He also had a propensity for adventure. He came to Palestine for the second time in late January 1948 and joined the Palmach. He participated in the battles of Castel and Katamon, and was wounded in the battle for Jerusalem—this time, quite seriously. He spent weeks in the hospital. It was there that David experienced his first great love: his nurse, Ahuva. He received his discharge from the army in the summer of 1949 and soon found a job as a teacher in an immigrants' camp near Rehovot. While in Germany, David had already taught Hebrew, Jewish history, and the Bible to youngsters in DP camps. Teaching would be David's profession in Israel for many years to follow. Teaching has been a great source of satisfaction to him.[16]

David's close family made aliyah from Brazil and arrived in Haifa in March 1950. Within a few months, he was teaching at a high school in Kiryat Haim, near Haifa, and had married Yehudit, whose family survived the war in Russia. The following year, he was offered a teaching position in English language and literature at the Afula high school. He began teaching there in the fall of 1952. I had already been a student there for a year. My first teacher of English was Kurt, from kibbutz Beit Alfa. I recall him as a tall, stooped man with a nose like an eagle's beak and a pronounced German accent. David Kochavi would be my English teacher for the next two years.

---

15   Ibid., 149–203, 208.
16   Ibid., 208.

I was eager to explore David's memories of Afula. "It was a nice and pleasant little town," he remembered. He distinctly recalled the school principal, Eliezer Kagan: "he was a highly educated man, very knowledgeable in literature and philosophy. A Socialist. A man of strength. I was very impressed." David and his wife lived in Afula Ilit, then a neighborhood recently built for new immigrants: "It was then the very beginning of that part of town. We lived in one of those very modest apartments. In winter the mud was knee-deep." We spoke for a while about some of the teachers who were his colleagues at my school, and about some of the students. When I asked David to sum up his two years in Afula, he commented, somewhat to my disappointment, "it was just an episode."[17]

I was able to track down several of my fellow students from Afula's high school. One of the oldest was Emda Or. I may have heard her name earlier, but it was only at Ben-Gurion University, where we both taught, that I first encountered her and learned her life story. Emda's mother, Esther, was born in Bialystok, Poland. Esther's parents, the Shulmeisters, purchased a plot in Afula and arrived there in 1925 with their two daughters. Esther was seven or eight at the time. They were one of those middle-class families of Polish Jews that settled in what was expected to become the urban center of the Valley. They opened a small coffee shop near the local train station. In time, they added a second floor, which served as a hotel. I was interested in the cultural background of Emda's family. "My grandparents spoke Yiddish at home and used to read the Yiddish newspaper *Forverts*. Grandma spoke to me in Yiddish and I spoke to her in Hebrew," Emda told me. Esther, after completing a few years at the local Mizrachi elementary school, had to quit her studies to help out at the hotel. Moshe, the man who would become Emda's father, arrived in Afula as a laborer and rented a room on the second floor. "Moshe was thirty-one and Esther fifteen. And they fell madly in love."[18] Moshe Herzig had arrived in 1919 to Palestine from Vienna, with his brother Shmulik. The Herzig brothers, though not party members, were definitely pro-Communist. In time, Shmulik married a young woman who was a Communist Party member. Both joined a group of young people who planned to settle in Soviet Birobidzhan. Shmulik, however,

---

17 Kochavi, interview.
18 Emda Or, interview by author, Beer Sheva, December 2009.

ended up in Moscow, where he eventually became an engineer. Moshe, who stayed in Palestine, worked for some years as a laborer, and following a bout of malaria sought medical treatment in Vienna. That's where he began to study engineering. The 1929 economic crisis in Europe forced him to return to Palestine. He never became an engineer.

Since Emda's grandparents strongly opposed the unusual love affair between Esther and Moshe, the couple eloped, married, and for a while lived in Jerusalem and then in Haifa, where Emda was born in 1932. They eventually settled in Kfar Yehezkel, near Afula, where Moshe found work as a mechanic. This is where Emda's younger brother, Yoram, was born in 1935. The family would make frequent trips to Afula by train: "The train came from Damascus. There were always lots of Arabs there, milling about at the train station. They all wore *abbayas*. Inside the train we saw Syrian Arabs wearing turbans. There were some British officers as well. It took about half an hour to reach Afula." Emda recalled, in particular, the train trips on Fridays: "On Friday afternoons all of Afula would dress up in their best clothes and stroll to the train station to welcome their guests for Shabbat. This scene repeated itself on Saturday afternoons, when the local families accompanied their departing guests. On those occasions Afula looked like a shtetl."[19] Within a few years, Emda's family moved to Afula and lived with her grandparents.

I was eager to hear whether Emda had any memories connected with the war and the Holocaust. "We definitely discussed it at school. Our homeroom teacher even decided once to make us feel hungry, like the Jews in the ghettos," she recalled. She also described a scene in the garden of the hotel near the train station: "Grandma didn't allow me to go down. I was glued to the window on the second floor. There was a crowd of those German Templars with a chaplain in front of them. And they were praying. They boarded the train that night and disappeared." What young Emda had witnessed was part of an exchange of German settlers for Jews from Mandatory Palestine who were stranded during the war in German-occupied Europe.[20] Emda vividly recalled British soldiers stationed in town at the time: "Afula was full of military men of all kinds. It looked like one big army camp. There were soldiers from India and from Pakistan. Some were wearing turbans. They sometimes also held marches with military bands. We kids would walk around their tents and get stamps. There were less joyous moments as well, like drunkenness. On the whole

---
19 Ibid.
20 Ibid.

these are powerful and happy childhood memories." Emda recalled some tense moments, too: people spoke of General Rommel conquering Egypt and reaching Palestine. For a while the family hotel was requisitioned by the British and served as a command post. Emda remembered seeing high-ranking officers. She also recalled how people around her kept informed of the shifting front lines, particularly those of the British and the Russian armies: "people adored the Red Army. They would sing Russian songs. These were our songs as well. We used to watch Russian films whenever they were screened in town. We were all excited about those Russian war heroes."[21]

I was eager to hear about Emda's schooling in Afula. "There was a small school in Kfar Yeladim in the mid-1940s. We were seven or eight kids to a grade. There was an encampment of the Arab Legion nearby, just across from the hospital," she told me. Emda's life was affected by the growing tension between Jews and Arabs. "There were several Arab villages near Afula and we expected trouble. Our school was even closed for a few months." Emda recalled a shelling of the town. "My grandma's hotel was converted into a military hospital." Emda, a youngster of fifteen, joined the *Gadna*, the paramilitary youth units. This is where she first met her future husband, Yosef. He was her Gadna counselor.

Yosef Averbuch, later Or, arrived in Palestine with his parents from Poland. His father was appointed as the administrator of the Davar newspaper branch in Afula. Yosef's younger brother, Theodore, was Emda's classmate. Yosef was mobilized and fought in the War of Independence. During the battle of Nazareth, he was seriously wounded. She recalled, "I started going out with Yosef right after the war. He was 19 and I was 16. He was still in constant pain from his wartime wounds. Still, he completed his matriculation exams and was offered a job as a teacher." Some of the demobilized young soldiers in Afula became friendly with senior high school girls. They would meet in private houses, talk, and dance. Sometimes, they went for hikes. Right after her graduation, in the summer of 1951, Emda married Yosef. She was eighteen and he was twenty-one. The modest wedding was held, of course, in the family hotel.[22]

Theodore Or, Yosef's younger brother and a lawyer by profession, served for some years as deputy chairman of the Supreme Court of Israel.

---

21 Ibid.
22 Ibid.

I interviewed him in his spacious and impressive law office, located on the forty-sixth floor of a skyscraper. He was quite official at first, but softened up as we delved into his childhood and adolescence in Afula. "As a matter of fact, this is the first time that I'm reminiscing about my Afula years," he said at one point. He had clear recollections of my uncle Zeev Bomze, perennially riding on his bike. He remembered also his onetime friend Sasha Paz, with whom he shared a room as a student in Jerusalem in the early 1950s.[23]

Teddy, as he is known to his friends, was born in 1934 in Poland and arrived with his parents and older brother, Yosef, in Mandatory Palestine two years later. His parents, Meir and Sara, had done an earlier stint in Palestine. Both had worked as young pioneers in the draining of the Hadera swamps. They returned to Poland when Sara fell ill with malaria and arrived in Palestine for the second time as a family of four.[24]

The Averbukhs settled first in Hadera, and quite soon afterwards, Meir was appointed as administrator of the Davar newspaper branch in Afula. Sara became a member of the local council. They were a typical small town Mapai—Labor Party—family: "My parents spoke, besides Hebrew, also Yiddish, Russian, and Polish. First we lived in a rented two-room apartment and later we moved to our own house in the Workers' Quarter." Teddy joined Emda's grade in the local school. He was very active in sports, mainly soccer and basketball. Like Emda, he recalled soldiers camping in town during the war: "I remember Australian soldiers wearing their special hats, as well as British policemen on their huge motorbikes." Theodore remembered the joy and the celebrations following the UN resolution in November 1947: "We had our own radio and followed the count. In a short while people were dancing in the main square."

I prodded Theodore for memories of his older brother Yosef:

> I adored him. He was very special, talented, good-looking and very popular with the girls. I recall one of his girlfriends, Bat-Ami, who rode with him on his bike. Couples used to spend time like that. When Yosef was wounded during the War of Independence, three different girlfriends came to visit him in the hospital at the same time. The most stormy romance was, of course, with Emda. She was then in the twelfth grade. They married following her graduation. That's why she never served in the Army.[25]

---

23 Theodore Or, interview by author, Ramat Gan, September 2014.
24 Ibid.
25 Ibid.

I was, of course, interested in Theodore's memories of our high school and its teachers. Like myself and my other Afula interviewees, his most impressive memory was that of Eliezer Kagan, who taught humanities and served as school principal. Kagan was a redhead with a mustache. He was quite different from the other teachers. He used to tell us that he had served as a policeman near the Dead Sea. "I recall him riding a motorbike," Teddy said. "We also knew that he was writing poetry. His was a very strong personality. Nobody fooled around in his classes. Everybody respected him."[26] I remember also some of the gossip about Eliezer's romances. One of these was with Aliza, the eldest daughter of Professor Fleischman, medical director of Valley Hospital. We imagined his girlfriends riding with him on his motorbike while he recited poetry.

Another famous public figure connected with Afula was Tommy Lapid. Lapid's name popped up quite naturally during my conversation with Theodore. At one time, Lapid had served as justice minister, and Theodore, as member of the Supreme Court. As Theodore told me, "whenever I met with Tommy we spoke about our Afula days. I recall Tommy's romance with my classmate Hava. He always spoke of her very favorably. I remember Hava as a very intelligent and good-looking young lady, though somewhat reserved." In one of his letters to Theodore, Tommy remarked, "who would have thought that Afula would produce a Justice Minister and a Deputy Chairman of the Supreme Court." Toward the end of our conversation, I asked Judge Or to try and look back on Afula of his childhood and adolescence. "I recall Afula fondly. Afula has always remained part of my life," he replied.[27]

Yosef "Tomi" Lapid, who would in time become a well-known Israeli media figure and politician, spent most of his army service near Afula. His son, Yair Lapid, likewise a media figure and a successful politician, described that short period in his father's life in his book *Memories after My Death*. Tomi was born as Tomislav Lampel, in Novi Sad, Yugoslavia, in 1931. He survived the Holocaust in the Budapest ghetto and arrived in Israel at the end of 1948, one day before his seventeenth birthday. He spoke Serbo-Croatian, Hungarian, and German, but he didn't know a word of Hebrew and had never belonged to any Zionist

---

26 Ibid.
27 Ibid.

youth organization. Yair must have heard on more than one occasion the tales of his father's first years in his new homeland. Imitating Tomi's distinctive brand of humor, Yair describes his father's arrival in Israel: "The sun rose behind a mountain. We didn't know that its name was Carmel. Its rays descended on a city. We didn't know that its name was Haifa. Somebody raised the Israeli flag." Tomi, though only seventeen, was offered the option of volunteering for the army, which he accepted on the spot. He was assigned to a group of youngsters his age, all from Yugoslavia. His impression of his military unit was that it was *"balagan"*—a complete mess. "The Company Commander would issue orders to the platoon commander in Hebrew. The platoon commander would translate them into German for Fischer, our squad leader, and Fischer would translate them for me into Hungarian. I was supposed to translate it into Serbo-Croatian, for the rest of my group. The result was that nobody carried out the orders." After two weeks of basic training, Tomi and his group were sent to kibbutz Yagur, not far from Haifa, to get acquainted with life on a kibbutz: "When we stepped into the kibbutz dining hall nobody greeted us. When later on they sang songs, we sat on the side and nobody approached us." They worked in various manual labor assignments for two weeks and returned to the army. All of them were then sent to jobs as auto mechanics and as trainees at an army base near Afula.[28]

The Israeli Defense Forces—IDF—base, which formerly served the Arab Legion, was located opposite the entrance to Valley Hospital. It is there that young Tomi met Hava, whose mother worked at the hospital. Hava Horowitz was born in 1934 in Vienna, to a religious Jewish family. Following the Anschluss, she fled with her parents to Italy. They survived partly in camps and partly in hiding. After the liberation in 1944, Hava's family lived in Jewish refugee camps until they were able to obtain immigration certificates from their relatives in Palestine. They reached Haifa in March 1945. Her father died shortly after their arrival. Hava's mother began work at Valley Hospital a few weeks later. She was in charge of the hospital laundry. This was apparently the first time that the eleven-year-old girl had been separated from her mother; she was sent to a religious youth village, where she lived and studied for the next three years. When I asked Hava—a retired professor of sociology and a successful author of biblical novels, about those first years in Israel—she replied, "these weren't very cheerful years." She was mostly

---

28 Yair Lapid, *Memories after My Death* [in Hebrew] (Jerusalem: Keter Books, 2010), 82–85, 90–92.

preoccupied with studying and reading. Hava rejoined her mother in the early summer of 1948. They shared a single room on the hospital premises. A diligent student, Hava was able to skip a year, and entered the Afula high school in the tenth grade.[29]

Hava's closest friends were two local teenage girls whose fathers worked at the hospital. "We were driven to school on a bus and used to hike back home," she recalled. They had a lively social life: "There were parties and dances. Either in the hospital dining hall or the nearby army base." When I asked her about Tomi, Hava was unable to recall specific details of their friendship. She did, however, remember that their conversations at first were in German; only later did they switch to speaking in Hebrew: "We discussed various books, such as those by Guy de Maupassant. Tomi was very 'European.' It was this European cultural background that made us feel good together." Tomi, as portrayed in his son's book, seems to have had more vivid memories of their friendship:

> I met Hava Horowitz at a party organized by Captain Shakhner. She and her mother arrived with a bunch of nurse students from the Hospital. I couldn't take my eyes off her. She was then an eleventh grader, blonde, gentle and good-looking. My Hebrew was quite bad, but I soon noticed that she spoke German with a Viennese accent. This was a rather innocent romance between adolescents. We would walk hand in hand and talk. It lasted for two years. What attracted me most to Hava was her Israeliness. I envied her and her teenage classmates their fluent Hebrew. It was from Hava that I learned about Israeli politics, about academia. She would translate novels for me from Hebrew, which I could not read or understand; she read and translated the newspaper headlines too. She introduced me to contemporary Israeli tunes and songs.[30]

As for their memories of Afula, both Tomi and Hava were not very impressed. Hava recalls the lone cinema in town and the occasional screenings of films in the hospital dining hall. "The town wasn't attractive. I looked forward to moving away to a big city." Tomi was more caustic: "I spent thirty-three months of my life in that hole. In the early fifties Afula was a gray and miserable town."[31]

---

29 Prof. Hava Halevi-Etzioni, interview by author, Tel Aviv, December 2015.
30 Lapid, *Memories after My Death*, 91, 96–97.
31 Ibid., 81–97; Halevi-Etzioni, interview.

When I arrived at Ben-Gurion University as a young lecturer in history in the early 1970s, I unexpectedly met Sasha Paz, who was teaching psychology. He was almost ten years older than me, and in Afula, we had never moved in the same circles. I did recall, however, that he was once a boyfriend of Maya Hershkowitz, my classmate Yair's older sister. Subsequently, at the university, we would meet from time to time, but it was only when I started to interview people who had lived in Afula that we sat down in his apartment and spoke for hours. I learned a lot about his personality. It turned out that Sasha had always been an outsider and a loner. He even once entertained the idea of becoming a monk.

Sasha was born in Galatz, Romania, in 1926. In his autobiographical novel, he describes his childhood among non-Jewish boys. His dominant memories of those years were of anti-Semitism, cruelty, and humiliation.[32] Still, throughout his adult life he continued to think and write about Christianity. He apparently sustained both feelings of attraction to and of repulsion from the Christian world. When I asked him about the war years he told me, "for me the war started in 1941 and ended in 1944." Part of that time Sasha had spent in labor camps. His father died in one of those camps. The adolescent protagonist in his novel goes through some extremely frightful and traumatic moments in similar situations.[33] It seems that the Holocaust years were carved into Sasha's persona, marking him for life. During his few months in Galatz and later in Bucharest, after the liberation, young Sasha was attracted to socialism and even to communism. In the end, however, he was drawn to a Zionist youth movement and decided to make aliyah and join a kibbutz.

Sasha left Romania shortly after the end of the war, and, via Hungary and Yugoslavia, arrived in Mandatory Palestine in the early summer of 1945. The illegal boat on which he traveled was apprehended by the British and was escorted all the way to the shore: "Around 4:00 in the morning we already could make out the Carmel. We arrived at the port of Haifa around 8:00 AM. My first impression was that of a tropical land: the blinding light, the hot weather; all of it was somewhat incomprehensible."[34] Sasha's group was escorted to the transit camp in Atlit, where he stayed for a few weeks. Ultimately, his group

---

32 Sasha Paz, *Il Monsignore* [in Hebrew] (Jerusalem: Carmel Publishers, 2006), 24–25.
33 Paz, *Il Monsignore*, passim; Sasha Paz, interview by author, Beer Sheva, February 2009.
34 Paz, interview.

reached kibbutz Beit Hashita in the Valley. He would often visit his married older brother, who lived in nearby Afula. Sasha would remain in Beit Hashita until 1950. His group of young immigrants was heterogeneous: "There were seven or eight young couples, some with children, all from Poland. Some single people, also from Poland. And then there were eight Hungarians and three Romanians, including myself."

The kibbutz and communal life were completely new to Sasha: "I saw a kibbutz dining hall for the first time in my life. For lodgings at first they put us in empty railroad wagons brought from the Afula railroad station, and later on in tents." Sasha and some others from his group were assigned to work in the fields and the cowshed. "We didn't mind. We were strong. Although we worked well, we encountered attitudes of condescension from some of the kibbutz members. I wasn't scared, though. At times I even looked for fights." Sasha mastered Hebrew within a short period and seemed to be self-confident. He wasn't even interested in a foster family, as some other young people in his group were. "I had a relationship with a married woman whose husband had left the kibbutz. She was a *tsabarit*—a native Israeli. We worked together in the cowshed." Work in the cowshed, the *refet*, was hard and demanding, and was the most respected kind of work in the kibbutzim.

The men in Sasha's group were drafted in the course of 1948 and fought in the War of Independence. When the war was over Sasha returned to the kibbutz and remained there until 1950, when he moved to Jerusalem. While in the kibbutz and in the army, Sasha would frequently visit Afula, and he made new friends there: "I liked Afula. It was a small and pleasant place. There were many educated young people. They read books. Some of them even knew foreign languages. We used to go to the movies together. There were two cinemas in Afula, Kuperman's cinema in the center, and Keytsi—the open-roof summer cinema, a bit further." One of Sasha's friends in Afula was Theodor Or. They were roommates later on in Jerusalem, when Teddy began to study law.

Sasha loved the Valley and its people. He even wrote a novel about it. As he told me, "People from nearby kibbutzim and from other settlements would arrive at the Afula grain depot on tractors and horses. They spoke about agriculture. They had real roots in this land. They believed in the Zionist dream and in its social message of equality. They weren't driven by greed." When Sasha met Maya Hershkowitz in Afula, she was twenty and had just completed her army service. He was six years older. Maya had been a classmate of Theodore and Emda, and Sasha would often spend time with them and their friends. All of that group were native-born sabras, graduates of the local high school. When

I asked Sasha about his friendship with Maya, he replied, "I wasn't ripe for a serious relationship. I was basically a loner with all kinds of fantasies."[35]

Yael Cohen and Naomi Edelstein were very close friends. Their families lived in the Workers' Quarter, a five-minutes' walk from each other. Both were of medium height: Yael, with straight black hair and a serious look on her face; and lively blond, blue-eyed Naomi. Both were one grade below me and socialized with boys in my class. I recall pleasant Friday evenings in the girls' homes. The get-togethers would usually start with Israeli-Russian songs, very popular in those years. There was a lot of talking and laughter. Sometimes, we would do the tango and the slow dance, with the curtains drawn as that kind of dancing wasn't accepted in certain parts of Israeli society in the early 1950s.

I had run into Yael and Naomi occasionally when all three of us were students at Hebrew University in the late 1950s. The next time I met with them was more than half a century later. Yael had specialized in education, and her American-born husband was a professor at the Weizmann Institute of Science. Naomi, a biologist, worked in a lab for many years. Her husband Dan, an engineer, worked at Rafael, the leading Israeli defense technology company. Yael, with her shapely gray hairdo, now looked quite distinguished. Naomi had aged considerably. I knew that she and Dan had lost a son in one of the Arab-Israeli wars; perhaps that was the reason.

Yael's parents were born in Poland a few years before the First World War. Both arrived in Palestine as Zionist pioneers when they were in their mid-twenties, a few years before the outbreak of the Second World War. Their group settled in Beit Hashita. Yael's father, Avraham Varum, soon made the decision that kibbutz life was not for him, and the couple moved to nearby Afula. A number of friends from the Klosowa pioneers' training farm in Poland were already living in town at the time, which made their adjustment less difficult. Avraham, who had studied accounting in Poland, took work as an accountant in the Afula flour mill, and in a short while, was given a senior position in the offices of the local *kupat cholim*, the Histadrut clinic. In a few years, he was appointed as the administrative director of the fast-growing Valley Hospital. He was also one of the founders of the Workers' Quarter.[36]

---

35 Ibid.
36 Yael Cohen-Yarom, interview by author, Rehovot, October 2013.

Yael was born in Valley Hospital in 1937. At the time, her family was living in a very modest apartment on Afula's Jerusalem Road. The family moved to Shkhunat Hapoalim—the Workers' Quarter—around the mid-forties. Yael studied in the local primary school and took piano lessons: "my piano teacher taught his lessons in a room at the old train station." She was eleven during the War of Independence. "During the air raid alarms we would run from our houses and lay in a nearby ditch. Once our neighbor Moser and his son used a machine gun to try to shoot down a plane," she told me.

I was eager to learn about Yael's memories of the war and the Holocaust. "Our neighbors kept their windows open so we could listen for news on their radio," Yael recalled. She has memories of her father's worries for his family, and especially of the day he learned that they had been killed: "We traveled to Tel Aviv to meet with an uncle who had arrived from Europe. My father listened to him and wept." Some of her father's surviving relatives came to Afula after the war, and her father helped them find jobs. Old-timers usually tried to help their families arriving from postwar Europe. My own uncle Zeev secured a driver's job at Electric Corporation for my uncle Vovo, who settled with his family in Afula in the fall of 1950.

I asked Yael about the absorption of youngsters from postwar Europe at school. She recalled, "Two girls, Elisheva and Malka, were placed in my class, sometime in 1949. Both sported permanents and wore earrings. That did them in. We never spoke with them about their past either." For some youngsters, such incidents could be traumatic. Elisheva would never wear earrings for the rest of her life.

I was particularly eager to hear about intimate friendships between the newcomers and the locals. The name of my closest friend, Nelu, popped up unexpectedly. It turned out that he wanted to be Yael's boyfriend. "He asked me to go out with him a few times. He was such a European gentleman—well mannered. It was quite pleasant but definitely out of place." Evidently, she turned him down.[37]

The most popular youth movement in Afula was *Hanoar Haoved*, affiliated with Mapai. Yael was a counselor there for a few years and even planned to join a kibbutz after her high-school graduation. Her parents convinced her to study at Hebrew University, instead. "It was a very tough decision. A sort of betrayal," she said. When I asked her to look back to her Afula childhood and adolescence she stated unhesitatingly "I'm actually a product of Afula in a most

---

37 Ibid.

positive sense. My years in Afula shaped my belief in hard work, loyalty to my family and friends, and love for the land. I've been to many places around the world. Still, I recall my Afula years as the happiest in my life."[38]

Naomi Edelstein, born in 1937, was one of the prettiest girls in our school. Her father, Yaakov, was a member of the Egged bus company and wore a cap that looked like an army officer's. Naomi's parents arrived in Palestine from Romania in the mid-1930s, lived first in Tel Aviv, and soon afterward moved to Afula. It had been rumored that work was to be had in that town. And, indeed, her father soon found employment there as a truck driver. Later, he took a position with the Egged bus company. During the War of Independence, he transported soldiers to the Negev and was absent from home for months.

I'd remembered that Naomi once had a boyfriend who was a young man from Poland. His name was Israel. Even now, I can distinctly picture his posture and his face. It stunned me that this pretty blue-eyed sabra girl had gone out with a new immigrant, and I was eager to learn more details. "We used to go to the movies and walk around town. He was one of those who survived the war in the Soviet Union," Naomi told me. "He was very intelligent and would talk about Communism and Soviet literature. My parents didn't approve of our friendship, mainly because of his Communist ideas." Naomi broke off the relationship after less than a year.

Her next boyfriend was Dan Simonov, my classmate. They married in the late 1950s. Naomi was quite outspoken about the attitudes of the sabras in her class towards the newcomers. "We were terrible. We made fun of their clothing and their manners. I feel guilty about it to this very day."[39]

There were two Dans in my class: Dan Simonov and Dan Mador. Their families belonged to the local small-town elite. Dan Simonov, who would later change his last name to Sinai, was the younger son of the boss of Electric Corporation's Afula branch. Dan Mador's father was a surgeon at Valley Hospital. I never met Dr. Mador. But Dan Simonov's father I saw quite often during the summer that I worked at Electric Corporation. This was immediately after I had left Merhavia. Simonov, senior, was a tall, gray-haired, impressive

---

38 Ibid.
39 Naomi Sinai-Edelstein, interview by author, Haifa, February 2014.

man, who usually wore British-style, knee-length khaki shorts. I was, of course, eager to learn more about him and his family.

The Simonovs stemmed from imperial Russia and had been well off before the 1917 Revolution. They were salt merchants. Their home in Sevastopol on the Black Sea was a meeting place for local and out-of-town Zionists. Among their guests were the Hebrew poet Shaul Tchernichovsky and the war hero Joseph Trumpeldor.

The eighteen-year-old Simonov, Dan's future father, arrived in Palestine in 1920 and joined *Gdud Haavoda*, the labor brigade. He found work as an employee of the fledgling Electric Corporation in the mid-twenties. Ten years later he was appointed as head of the Afula branch. Dan's mother was from Rovno and was a graduate of the local Hebrew Tarbut high school. According to Dan, his parents spoke Hebrew with their sons and Russian to each other. Dan's father had served in the British Army during the Second World War. He saw action in Italy and in Belgium, and was involved in the liberation of the Bergen-Belsen concentration camp. At the request of Yokheved Barakan from Afula, Dan's father drove her surviving sister from Bergen-Belsen to France; from there, she left for Palestine. I asked Dan if he had memories of the War of Independence. He was then a boy of twelve. One dramatic event was clearly etched in his mind: "There was a horrible event in Vadi Ara. An Electric Corporation vehicle from Afula was attacked by Arab villagers. One man was killed on the spot and another was severely wounded and died later in the Valley Hospital. I remember it clearly. This was my first funeral."[40]

We started talking about our class. "There was a mix of local youngsters and the newcomers—Shimon, Nelu, Dudu, Esther and Hinda. Dudu and Nelu, who both came from Romania, spouted Communist ideology. At first we had heated arguments; they mellowed after a while." I recall that Nelu once took me to a man who lived in one of the local maabarot and who was apparently a Communist. We discussed politics with him, but there was no follow up. Dan did not recall anything condescending in the attitudes of the sabras in our class toward the newcomers, except during arguments over politics.[41] When I try to square Dan's account of these relations between the locals and the newcomers with that of Yael and Naomi, it seems that age made a considerable difference. In the higher grades, the attitudes seem to have been more balanced.

---

40   Dan Sinai, interview by author, Haifa, February 2014.
41   Ibid.

I knew that Dan Mador, whose original last name was Mendershausen, had come from an upper middle-class German-Jewish family. We were classmates in Afula for three years, and we were also assigned to the same company during our basic military training. He appears in some of my old army photos. I learned much more about him and his family when I interviewed him sixty years later. Dan's father, Alfred-Abraham, had been born in Berlin at the turn of the nineteenth century and served in the German Army during the First World War. He studied medicine in the 1920s and married in 1933. Following our interview, Dan sent me a presentation he had prepared for his mother's one-hundredth birthday. Erna, born in 1906, had three siblings. Her older brother served in the army during the First World War. Erna studied in a school for girls, and as the photos indicate, she had a happy childhood and adolescence. The family had a busy social life and went on hikes and picnics. Erna played the piano and the mandolin. At times, they went skiing in Austria and on trips farther away. One photo shows young Erna on the Piazza San Marco in Venice.[42]

Dan's parents immigrated to Palestine in the summer of 1933 and a year later settled in Afula. Dr. Mendershausen worked for the Histadrut local clinic as a general practitioner and treated people not only in town but also around the Valley. He drove a motorcycle but at times had to use a mule as his means of transportation. He always carried a gun. Dr. Mendershausen was appointed to head the surgery department at Valley Hospital in 1941, and the family moved up to the hospital grounds. According to Dan, there were just a few other kids there and they would take the bus to attend school in Afula. One of Dan's happiest childhood memories was connected with the Glider's Club, run by the Haganah and the Palmach, on the slopes of Giv'at Hamoreh. He used to watch the gliders for hours: "once, Dani Schapiro, the gliding instructor, took me along with him on a glider."[43]

My interview with Dudu Feibish, husband of my cousin Ora and our classmate in Afula's high school, took place in somewhat bizarre circumstances. They had been living permanently in Paris for many years. Their daughter, Bilha, who lived in Tel Aviv, had just passed away and I went to the *shiva*—the gather-

---

42 DVD presentation by Dan Mador on the occasion of his mother's one-hundredth birthday. In the author's possession.
43 Dan Mador, interview by author, Haifa, March 2014.

ing for mourners—in her apartment, where I met them. I tried to talk to Ora, but her advanced dementia, from which she had been suffering for the last few years, made it impossible. We were sitting and conversing casually. After a while, I took the chance of asking Dudu whether he recalled his adolescence in Afula. To my surprise, he agreed to answer my questions. Our talk about that distant past enlivened somewhat the somber mood.

It turned out that Dudu and his parents had arrived in Israel in September 1950. They were part of the massive immigration of Romanian Jews. Dudu had been very gifted in math and music since his childhood. In Romania, he attended a school that emphasized math and physics; he also played the accordion. I asked Dudu about his first impressions of Afula. He told me, "They brought us straight from Shaar Aliya to *maabara B*, near Afula, on the way to the Valley Hospital, on the left side of the road, out in the fields. The new immigrants were mostly from Iraq, Yemen, and Romania and lived in tents. It was terribly hot during the summer and freezing cold in the winter. A number of outhouses were scattered among the tents. And there was also a tiny food shop—a *makolet*. I went daily to the school in the nearby Workers' Quarter, mostly on foot."[44] This must have been in the fall of 1950. Dudu was assigned to the class of my cousin Ora. I would join that class a year later. Dudu had vague memories of an amateur theater group of newcomers that included his countryman Yaakov Bodo: "I joined the group; we performed in *Kolron*, Afula's newly built 'House of Culture.'"

I was eager to hear about Dudu's encounter with the locals. He told me about his first day in school: "I was dressed in a suit and wore a cap. I took it off and said '*bonjour*.' They burst out laughing. All those suntanned boys and girls, wearing shorts, looked to me like barbarians. I couldn't speak any Hebrew. Israel Matzner, the math teacher, spoke to me in Yiddish."[45]

Dudu quickly learned Hebrew and made friends with some of the young people in town. His parents bought him an accordion and he started playing it on various occasions. "I'd play at weddings, on army bases and in other places. This way I could make some money." Compared with other immigrant youths Dudu was unusually successful in forming social contacts. He made it a point not to stick with the newcomer crowd. "It's easy for me to get friendly with people," he said.

---

44 Dudu Feibish, interview by author, Tel Aviv, May 2016.
45 Ibid.

One of his new friends invited him to a dancing party at Valley Hospital. "I came dressed in a suit and tie, and again people were laughing. I took off the tie and the jacket and the laughter stopped. I've been accepted. Some of these people even became close friends. It all happened quite naturally," he recalled. Dudu's mother found a job at the hospital, and his father first worked as a manual laborer and later opened a food stand. Dudu was inducted into the army in 1952, just before his eighteenth birthday: "my father accompanied me to the bus, in the center of town, and was in tears." At that time, Dudu was already going steady with my sabra cousin Ora. They married in 1955. Dudu was then barely twenty-one; and Ora, nineteen. In his later life, Dudu had a very successful career as an aeronautical engineer in the Dassault Airplane Company in France. When I asked him to look back on Afula in the 1950s, he described it as a nice little town: "these were some of the most pleasant years of my life."[46]

Nira Bleiberg was another classmate from Afula. I recalled her as pleasant and good looking, and a close friend of Ora. The two couples—Ora and Dudu, and Nira and Yoram—used to spend many hours together. I hadn't seen Nira since our school days. When I interviewed her sixty years later, she had changed a lot, but was still a very pleasant person. Yoram's framed picture as a young man was placed right near the coffee table at which were sitting. He had died some twenty years earlier and Nira had never remarried.

Nira's parents, the Bleibergs, had come from eastern Galicia: her father, Mates, was from Boryslaw, known for its oil deposits; and her mother, Regina, was from a small town near Kolomyja. Both arrived in Palestine in the early 1930s. They married and settled in Afula. A number of Mates's friends from Boryslaw were already living and working in Afula at that time. "There was a whole company from Boryslaw there, and in fact they became my substitute family," Nira recalled.[47] Since Mates had some former experience in oil drilling, he started drilling wells in Palestine. After an accident, he could no longer work as a manual laborer, and the family opened a Tnuva dairy restaurant. Nira was born in Valley Hospital in 1936. She recalled being a bookworm, reading Karl May and Jules Verne. Like her teenage girlfriends, she liked to watch

---

46 Ibid.
47 Nira Hardof-Bleiberg, interview by author, Netanya, August 2011.

films: "We adored film-stars. In Ora's house they had a subscription to *Mishmar Layeladim* and in mine for *Davar Layeladim*—two children's journals. Both carried photos of film-stars. We used to cut them out and paste them in special copybooks. My girlfriend Ofra used to travel during the summer vacations to Tel Aviv. She'd always tell me about the films she'd seen there. It was almost like watching them."

I wanted to stir up some of Nira's memories of high school. As she remembered, "the most colorful personality there was our principle, Eliezer Kagan. He was a redhead. Students used to gossip about him a lot. He was divorced and had girlfriends. He also played the violin on various festive occasions, and drove a motorcycle. He was an outstanding teacher as well. He was special and I adored him. All of us did."[48]

Boy-girl socialization issues were also on my mind. Why was Dudu more accepted by the locals, the girls in particular, than other newcomers like myself? Nira tried to explain, "He was a good-looking guy and quite self-confident. He told us about his past experience with girls. He also played the accordion. He impressed us. And it was Ora who ended up as his girlfriend. She was lucky indeed." I was, of course, interested in hearing about my cousin Ora, who regretfully I could not interview. It turned out that Nira and Ora had been very close friends for decades:

> Zeev Bomze brought her to Afula from kibbutz Merhavia. We met first at Shula's. Shula's father and Bomze worked together at Electric Corporation. And they were like family. The whole thing seemed to me quite mysterious. Here was this orphan girl without a mother, living on a kibbutz, where she had an aunt, Pnina, Zeev's sister. A *yaldat khutz*. She comes to Afula and we become friends. Our friendship solidified at age fifteen or sixteen, when we started to have boyfriends and spend time together.

I also learned a thing or two from Nira about how couples formed:

> It started in the lower grades. All of us used to spend our Friday evenings at the youth movement. A boy would say "you are my girlfriend" or a girl would say "you are my boyfriend," and it might last for a week or two. And then new couples popped up. There were times that I changed boyfriends every two weeks. It wasn't serious. It was rather childish. I started going

---

48 Ibid.

out with Yoram sometime during the summer of 1951. I sat with a friend on a bench in the Palm-Trees Boulevard in the center of town. Suddenly Yoram arrived on his bicycle, on his way to play basketball or volleyball and we started chatting and the rest is history.[49]

It seems that couples would spend time mostly within their wider "circle" of friends, the *hevreh*. The boys were usually a year or two older than the girls. I asked Nira again about Ora, with whom they shared the same circle of friends. She recalled, "Ora had always suitors. She is an attractive woman even today. She was always lively and full of zest—*pilpel*. She and Dudu used to argue and quarrel. Most of us didn't believe this couple would last." Nira reminded me what a nuisance Ora could be at times to our teachers: "She once asked David Kochavi, our English teacher, 'How old are you?' and he said '36.' And then Ora said 'It can't be. You must be older.' She actually made him show us his ID. That fit your cousin Ora perfectly."[50]

Figure 3.1 Afula in the 1920s.

---

49 Ibid.
50 Ibid.

Figure 3.2 The Workers' Quarter in Afula in the 1940s.

Figure 3.3 First of May parade in Afula in the late 1940s.

Figure 3.4 Independence Day in Afula, May 1949.

Figure 3.5 The author in front of his apartment in Afula, 1952.

Figure 3.6 High school students in Afula. Nelu is standing between the two girls; the author is kneeling on the right.

Figure 3.7 The author with Nelu and a girlfriend.

Figure 3.8 Classmates. *Bottom row*: Ora Bomze, second from left; Nira Bleiberg, third from left. *Top row*: Dan Mador, first from left; Yair Hershkowitz, second from left; the author, third from left; Dan Simonov, fourth from left; Nelu, sixth from left.

CHAPTER 4

Training Base Four

I was inducted into the Israeli Army on August 24, 1954, just a few weeks after completing my *bagrut*—matriculation exams. We were taken on a bus from the recruiting station in Afula to the IDF induction center in Tzrifin, or "Sarafand," as the British called it. We all were in high spirits. This mood soon changed when they put us on the recruits' transmission belt. We were given extremely short haircuts and were issued khaki clothing that mostly didn't fit. The first night in the army was spent in an open tent. We barely slept. A harsh shrieking voice woke us early in the morning. Okhana, a lance corporal, apparently of Iraqi or Moroccan origin, drilled us for hours on end. A day or two later we were transferred to the nearby "Bahad-4": Training Base Four or TB-4. Each of us was given a personal army number. Mine was 305796: I can recite it instantly even today. We were also issued personal rifles, our closest companions for the next two months.

Tzrifin, located between Rishon LeZion and Beer Yaakov, was the site of numerous IDF bases, one of the largest being TB-4: the principal training base for male infantry recruits. Some training programs were meant for recruits with a low physical profile, referred to as *kaf lamed* or *kosher lakuy*: grade-B soldiers. It wasn't a thing to brag about in those days. The 1950s were the years of mass immigration to Israel, and these military training programs served as a melting pot for young immigrants. For many, it was the first time that they had lived and trained together with Israeli-born high-school graduates. Those graduates were drafted mostly in August and November, which is why the basic training courses that began then consisted of the most educated draftees. Not all of the Israeli-born recruits were able to adjust to their less educated peers. According to one graduate, "the people I live with aren't the greatest. More than half come from Kurdistan, some of them can't even sign their names."[1] The prevailing attitude of the instructors, mostly corporals and sergeants, was that only

---

1 Letter from Bahad-4, August 18, 1957, accessed January 7, 2015, http://news.nana10.co.il/Article.

by breaking the civilian spirit of the recruits would they be turned into real soldiers. Thus, another high school graduate remarked in a letter, "it's unnerving sometimes when a young man, not much older than myself, who's never heard of Pythagoras or Thomas Mann, is yelling at me and forcing me to do whatever he fancies, only because of the two stripes on his sleeve."[2] The commander of TB-4 in the early and mid-1950s was Lieutenant Colonel Dov Yirmiyah, whose parents were among the founders of Nahalal in Jezreel Valley. He was a contemporary of another man from Nahalal, Moshe Dayan. Yirmiyah was a member of the Haganah and served in the British Army during the Second World War. His future wife, Hadassah Mor, was stationed in TB-4 and served as Yirmiyah's secretary. Later, Hadassah became Dayan's lover. For years, Yirmiyah voiced bitter charges and accusations against Dayan.

Yirmiyah was asked to evaluate the recruits. In a report written in 1951, he concentrates on the oriental draftees, whom he referred to as "primitives." He spoke of three groups, defined by their countries of origin. Group A: Turks, Moroccans, Egyptians (sensible, learn by imitation, have a positive attitude toward weapons, scared at first to use live ammunition, get used to it in time). Group B: Iraqis and Iranians (mentally inferior, uncomprehending, see weapons at first as toys, cowardly, scared to shoot, afraid of the dark, have an inferiority complex, love parades). Group C: Yemenites (mentally inferior, have a respectful attitude towards weapons, learn by imitation, diligent, sectarian oriented). These traces of prejudice and stigma notwithstanding, the report described some of the real problems that prevailed in the army in the early 1950s. Social and cultural encounters between conscripts of widely different origins and the sabras resulted in considerable conflicts. In time, however, a certain measure of successful integration was reached. The turning point came, apparently, in 1953. Junior instructors in training bases were ordered to not use force or abusive language towards trainees. These new orders took time to implement.[3]

Yehoshua Kenaz, who would become one of Israel's most prominent writers, was a recruit at TB-4 in the summer of 1955, exactly one year after me. His epic novel *Infiltration* conveys in a masterly manner the realities and emotions that prevailed in the training of grade-B soldiers. The book opens with a most cruel and frightening exercise, *horadat zakif* or the "silencing of a sentry":

---

2 Letter from Bahad-4.
3 Sagi Turgan, "Training Combat: Leadership in the IDF, 1949–1956" [in Hebrew] (PhD diss., Hebrew University, 2008), passim.

> I fell on Micky's hand and bent it until I forced him down. When I placed the crook of my arm where his shoulder joins his neck, to look for the artery, the instructor, having apparently lost all faith in me, crouched down beside me, tightened my grip on the exact spot, and squeezed my elbow to increase the pressure. Micky beat his feet twice on the ground. "Don't let go," said the instructor as he increased his pressure on my elbow. Micky fell, swooning and extremely heavy, on my arm. I averted my eyes so as not to see his face.[4]

This scene was a most dramatic example of breaking the civilian spirit of both recruits, the "sentry" and his "silencer."

I read *Infiltration* twice. The first time was right after its publication in 1986; the second was recently, in the course of writing this book. I wanted to refresh my memories of TB-4. Some scenes that evoked the special ambiance of that place and time were powerful and moving. One memory summoned up mixed feelings: that of the week-long, mind-numbing exercises for the commanding officer's parades that were held on Friday mornings, before we were issued our leaves. "In the terrible heat of the end of summer," writes Kenaz,

> we marched back and forth, endlessly repeating the same movements over and over again, shouldering and presenting and ordering arms, closing ranks and opening ranks and closing them again in time to the commands yelled at us. [. . .] It was only the next morning, in the fever of preparation and excitement, fear and happiness, that things fell into place. One by one the companies and platoons marched onto the parade grounds and fell in around three of its sides. The process of marching on and falling in, although it was slow and complicated, became clearer and clearer, as the parade ground filled up, and all the companies and platoons took up their places.[5]

I, too, liked those moments when I could feel part of something large and visually pleasing. Perhaps those feelings of pride and pleasure harkened back to my childhood in prewar Poland when I was thrilled to watch military parades and listen to military bands.

---

4 Kenaz, *Infiltration*, 17 (South Royalton, VT: Zoland Books, 2003).
5 Ibid., 66–67.

At times, the instructors tried, often successfully, to mix reality with fantasy. As part of a night maneuver the instructor would say, "this is no longer an exercise. From now on this is for real. This is a true combat operation. Intelligence has received information that gangs of *fedayeen* are prowling round here at night. They may be over there, opposite us, they may be hiding in the orange grove."[6] The most frightening and shameful event that I remember was the "Infiltration Exercise." But Kenaz's description of his infiltration exercise seems even more terrifying: "Suddenly there was a sound of a shot, and then another one. Bullets began whistling over our heads and flying past us. I hugged the ground with my body and buried my face in my hands. [. . .] Zero-Zero shouted behind me: 'Madmen! They want to kill us! What's wrong with them? Madmen! Madmen!'"[7] It later turned out that these were blanks. In my case they didn't use bullets, but bayonets. Each of us was given a message on a tiny scrap of paper which we were supposed to hide and deliver beyond "enemy lines." As I was running half bent among the bushes, somebody sprang at me, pushed me down, touched my neck with his bayonet, yelled, and demanded the scrap of paper. Though I knew it was an exercise, I still gave it to him.

The protagonist of Kenaz's novel is in fact the whole platoon of grade-B recruits. The recruits are strangers to each other, all from different countries of origin; even the sabras have varying backgrounds: they come from assorted cities, villages, and kibbutzim. The platoon collective represents Israeli society at large in the mid-fifties. But by contrast with the "outside," in TB-4, they are continuously pressed into the same space, constantly under tremendous pressure, and very often treated by their instructors with contempt. They are constantly humiliated. The fact that they are grade-B soldiers breeds an inferiority complex in some of them.[8]

When I attempt to compare the memory of my specific platoon with the one described by Kenaz, it seems I was lucky. Or, perhaps Kenaz purposely exaggerated the behavior and situations to dramatize the conditions of basic training. I recall several instructors. Some were tougher than others. Two seemed to be immigrants, and they were the worst. One was a sabra, and he was more lenient and friendly. I must have forgotten a lot. Kenaz wrote his book thirty years after his experiences in TB-4. I'm trying to recall my training from a distance of over six decades. But it seems that people in my platoon were,

---

6   Ibid., 416.
7   Ibid., 492–94.
8   Nitza Ben Dov, *War Lives: On the Army, Revenge, Grief, and the Consciousness of War in Israeli Fiction* [in Hebrew] (Jerusalem: Shocken Publishing House, 2016), 143–79.

on the whole, nicer than those in his account. Most of the time, I managed to do what we were asked to. Still, there were some exceptions. Once, I evaded a strenuous night exercise by pretending to have a toothache. On the whole, though, I never felt inferior to the others. On the other hand, unlike some recruits, I never attempted to become a grade-A soldier and never dreamt of real combat. I always knew that I was not paratrooper material and that I would end up in a desk job.

Another, rather cheerful, memory of my days in basic training that has remained with me for over sixty years is the Company D song, written and composed for the final celebration event of our course. The melody I can still hum and the song's refrain I can clearly recall:

> Our company, Company D
> Will never fail or disappoint,
> Its health profile is indeed B
> But its spirit is the point.

This song has been always connected in my mind with the name of Poldi Shatzman, a popular Israeli composer who survived the Holocaust in Romania and immigrated to Israel in 1949. He could not have been one of us in Company D, since he was much older, but it is possible that he was asked to write the music.

What was the IDF, in fact, like in the early 1950s? The massive immigration to Israel had a tremendous impact on the army, as it did on the country as a whole. For example, out of close to 19,000 recruits between April 1950 and March 1951, only fourteen percent were sabras; about fifty-six percent had lived in Israel fewer than three years. These proportions were to shift dramatically within just a few years, once the influx of new immigrants ebbed. In the period between April 1954 and March 1955, close to forty percent of the draftees were sabras, while immigrants who had lived in Israel for more than four years comprised around fifty percent of the recruits. Thus, by the mid-1950s, the joint category of sabras and "old immigrants" among the draftees reached ninety percent. That ended the period in which new immigrants predominated among the army's draftees.

The immigrant recruits in the IDF of the early 1950s came from a variety of countries. Of the draftees between October 1952 and March 1953, over thirteen percent came from Iraq, over ten percent from Morocco, around eleven percent from Romania, and close to six percent from Poland. Draftees from Arab countries reached fifty-one percent. Every second recruit was an oriental Jew. The education of these recruits varied according to their countries of origin. Among those originating in North Africa, close to fifteen percent were illiterate. Nearly seventy percent of the letters written by soldiers in 1951 were in languages other than Hebrew. Instruction in Hebrew for the recruits was given a high priority. Thus, the percentage of letters written in Hebrew in the army rose to eighty-six percent in 1954. The number of high-school graduates among the recruits rose from 802 in 1948 to 2,179 in 1954.[9]

I have also tried to gain a better understanding of the social and political context of mid-1950s Israel, as well as of the security considerations that prevailed at the time. The Israeli Army, from its very inception, was thought to serve a most significant function in nation building and in merging the various sectors of Israeli society, especially the young ones, during the period of mass immigration. Politically, Israel in general and the army in particular bore, in those years, the distinctive imprint of two figures: David Ben-Gurion and Moshe Dayan. Although Ben-Gurion resigned as prime minister in December 1953, he appointed his close political ally Moshe Dayan as chief of staff just before leaving for Sde Boker in the Negev. Dayan would head the army until 1957, and his military and security concepts left a clear mark on it. Both Ben-Gurion and Dayan openly thwarted the moderate policies of Prime Minister Moshe Sharett. Both were strong proponents of retaliatory raids against Arab infiltrators. It was Dayan, in particular, who made efforts to build up IDF's fighting spirit. Military raids into enemy territory were considered a highly effective method of shaping that spirit. An activist climate prevailed in some leading units—particularly in Commando Unit 101, under the leadership of Ariel Sharon, established in the summer of 1953. This unit would become the nucleus of Paratroopers' Battalion 890, under Sharon's command.[10] A total of eleven raids were conducted throughout 1954. Operation "Black Arrow," in Gaza in February 1955, resulted in the death of eight paratroopers, among them Ehud Shachar from Merhavia, one of my Gefen peers. This was nearly three years after I had left the kibbutz. The fighting spirit and the raids into Jordanian

---

9 Turgan, "Training Combat," 35–51; Sagi Turgan, "Battle Leadership: The Commander Image in the IDF and Its Origin" [in Hebrew] (master's thesis, Hebrew University, 2001), 83.
10 Amos Perlmutter, *Military and Politics in Israel: Nation-Building and Role Expansion* (London: Frank Cass, 1969), 64, 85–86; Yoram Peri, *Between Battles and Ballots: Israeli Military in Politics* (Cambridge: Cambridge University Press, 1983), 237.

and Egyptian territory had far-reaching effects on the IDF as a whole. The paratrooper quickly turned into a kind of a model soldier. People, particularly the young, told and retold stories of daring acts of bravery and sacrifice. The red beret and high military boots of the paratroopers became a status symbol.

Basic military training, whenever and wherever it takes place, is a stressful period in any young man's life. I have tried to examine and understand the specifics of basic military training in Israel in the mid-1950s, and especially of basic training of grade-B soldiers—the kaf lameds. Any young recruit is challenged by the sudden transition from a civilian life to the unfamiliar reality of the military. The first days are the most challenging. The principal features of the new situation are humiliation, isolation, lack of privacy, and physical and psychological pressure. The recruit is usually thrown into an unfamiliar social milieu to which he must adapt. He becomes part of his training unit and spends days and nights with total strangers. There is, of course, also the stressful and highly hierarchical relationship between the junior instructors and their trainees. Young men face previously unknown situations in which they are required to be aggressive and violent.[11]

I also sought documentary evidence of my own basic training in the army. A significant resource has been the IDF Archive, located not far from the site where TB-4 used to be. I immersed myself in the statistics, orders, and routines of TB-4. Among other things, I wanted to see whether these old documents supported my memories and those of my interviewees.

According to the plan for the basic training course of August 1954 at TB-4, the army expected 1,125 recruits. Of these, 625 would be trained as combat soldiers. 560 would go through Grade-B training: I would be one of them.[12]

Each platoon of recruits consisted of about fifty men; three platoons made a company. Platoons were usually divided into three squads. Examining a photo of my own squad marching in line while training in the sands of Nebi Rubin, I counted seventeen men. I was, of course, eager to identify the name of our company commander—the most senior officer with whom I came into contact—and the names of our instructors. The commander's name, indeed, appeared on numerous documents: it was Lieutenant Moshe Shakuf. I vaguely recall that he was from Bulgaria. In a photo I've kept all these years he looks

---

11 Nava Guttman, "Processes of Coping and Adaptation in Stress" [in Hebrew] (master's thesis, Bar-Ilan University, 1989), 15; Orit Taubman, "Hardiness, Mental Health and Coping Processes during Basic Military Training" [in Hebrew] (master's thesis, Bar-Ilan University, 1993), 5–7.

12 Letter, IDF Chief Adjutancy, April 20, 1954, IDF Archive, File 1-301/1956.

quite handsome and impressive in his officer's uniform. I wanted very much to meet him again. I looked through several telephone books and made a few calls: to no avail. He may be dead by now. As for the junior instructors of Company D I found such names as Zvi Yehuda and Meir Zilberman. To my disappointment, only one name triggered a definite memory, that of lance corporal Shmuel Breit. He was slightly older than the others and more humane. Other instructors barked their orders at us and made us feel incompetent and stupid.

Another name I found in a file was that of Captain Dr. Khava Perlstein, the medical officer of the base. She must have looked like a man. Rumor had it that when scolding recruits for not shaving properly, she would yell at them, "if I can shave daily, why can't you?" I went on sick leave a number of times. I recall, somewhat shamefully, that on one occasion I faked being ill so as to evade a strenuous night march.

We used to gossip about our instructors and, at times, even curse them in their absence. It was, therefore, quite a revelation for me to find a letter written by the base commander to his superiors, urging them to replace some of the instructors: "Some of the young instructors become emotionally tense from the difficulties of their work and due to the low quality of the recruits. This results at times in their harsh treatment of the recruits."[13]

In the IDF archive, I found many pages with details of the daily military training plans signed by Company Commander Moshe Shakuf. A typical training day included physical exercises, rifle instruction, and drills. Later, we would practice bayonet warfare and learn the specifics of the machine gun. I recall stabbing sacks with straw to the accompaniment of ear-rending shouts. It was said we would have to stab sacks with live cats inside them, but this never actually happened. One of the high points was shooting with live ammunition. The exciting and frightening infiltration exercise was usually held in the last week of the training course.

The most serious and strenuous training took place outside the Tzrifin military compound, in the sands of Nebi Rubin. This was a large area of sand dunes west of Tzrifin and along the shore of the Mediterranean. In a task order issued in mid-September 1954, our company commander, Moshe Shakuf, described it as "a sandy area with scant vegetation which serves at times for the transit of Arab infiltrators. They cross the border for the purpose of robbery,

---

13   Letter, Lieutenant Colonel Dov Yirmiyah, August 1, 1954, IDF Archive, File 111-301/1956.

murder and espionage."[14] In these sand dunes, we practiced putting on camouflage, advancing at night, observation, and reconnaissance. We also did a lot of rifle shooting with live ammunition. One of the strict security instructions was that "every soldier must carry his rifle at all times and sleep with it at night." I vaguely recall that during one of the midday marches in the sand I was barely able to carry my rifle; someone must have carried it for me for a while.

Discipline and drilling practices in the Israeli Army in the mid-1950s were still influenced by British military tradition. There were endless hours of marching, turning, saluting, falling out, and falling in. The recruits' shacks were inspected on a daily basis. A document from the summer of 1954 gave new instructions for the bed arrangements: "In re Friday inspections: shoes must not be placed on top of the bed. They are to be placed under the bed with the back of the shoe leaning against the foot of the bed."[15]

After many attempts I was able to reestablish contact with two people who were in my platoon.

Yaakov Guterman is a well-known Israeli illustrator and educator. He often accompanies Israeli youth groups to Poland. Like myself, he is a child survivor. We did basic training together in the summer of 1954, and afterwards, our paths diverged for many years. I recall Yaakov as a friendly and outgoing fellow. His bed was almost opposite mine in the long and narrow wooden army shack. I was aware at the time that he was a kibbutznik and an artist. Years later, I happened to see him on TV. He was talking about his son Raz, killed during the first days of the Lebanon War in June 1982. I had vaguely known of Guterman's recurring critiques and diatribes against the Israeli leadership, directed mainly at Begin and Sharon, for causing the loss of lives of young Israelis in an unnecessary war. His appearance on TV triggered some old memories, and the following day I sent him a photo from our time on Training Base Four. In it, we are marching in the sands of Nebi Rubin. Guterman is somewhere in the middle of the line and I'm almost at its end. I had met him fleetingly on a number of occasions. But it was only when I interviewed him in his home in 2014 that I immersed myself into his biography. We sat for hours and reminisced about our army days, looking through dozens of old photos. I learned that there was

---

14 Task Order, September 16, 1954, IDF Archive, File 111–301/1956.
15 File 506–407/1957.

something besides our common army past that linked us: our Polish origins and our mutual interest in Polish culture.

Yaakov Guterman is the same age as me. He was born in April 1935 in Plock, in central Poland, and was the only child to his young, secular, middle-class Jewish parents. Both were communist sympathizers. Yaakov's happy prewar childhood came to an end in early September 1939, when the Germans occupied the city. Within a few weeks, the family had moved from their pleasant, comfortable apartment into a single shabby room in the local ghetto. His father was severely wounded in one of the first German raids. When the Plock ghetto was liquidated in February 1941, the Gutermans lived in hiding in several towns, assisted by friendly Poles. But hostile Poles posed a deadly danger. Young Yaakov became soon Staszek and learned Christian prayers by heart. The family ended up in Warsaw. While in hiding, Yaakov's father, Simcha, wrote hundreds of pages about the Jewish community in Plock and its tragic fate. The long strips of paper filled with tiny letters were stacked into empty bottles and hidden in various locations. Simcha joined the 1944 Polish uprising in Warsaw and died in battle. Yaakov and his mother survived.[16]

Yaakov and his mother, like some of the few other local survivors, returned to Plock in early 1945. He had serious health problems and was sent to convalesce at a Jewish children's home in Rabka, near Zakopane, at the foot of the Tatra Mountains. He recalled how he and his friends "learned from one day to the next how to be children again." When the place was shut down following an anti-Semitic incident, Yaakov returned to Plock, where he lived with his mother and stepfather in a tiny one-room apartment. They immigrated to Israel in the summer of 1950 and arrived at Haifa on board the *Galila*. The family lived for a time in various immigrants' camps, finally moving into a tiny apartment in an immigrants' housing facility in Acre. Yaakov spent two years in a local high school and then continued his education in kibbutz Ein Harod, in the Valley. It is from there that he was drafted to Training Base Four in the summer of 1954.[17]

I invited Yaakov Guterman to my eightieth birthday party; unfortunately, he could not attend. Instead, he sent me a letter summarizing his memories of Training Base Four:

> It's the summer of 1954. It's Sarafand: the huge military base that the British abandoned. It's busy as a beehive. Our company, "Company

---

16 Yaakov Guterman, introduction to *Leaves out of the Fire* [in Hebrew], by Simcha Guterman (Jerusalem and Tel Aviv: Yad Vashem and Moreshet Publishers, 2004), 13–36.
17 Guterman, *Leaves out of the Fire*, 282–84.

D," consists of conscripts from all over the country. Their medical records, according to the health inspection committee, have made them Grade-B soldiers, who can't join combat units. Still, our tough Company Commander consistently refuses to accept this fact. For weeks on end he tries to turn us into real fighters. We get up at 5 am each day, clean our long military shack, the home of sixty or so recruits; we shovel the soil around the nearby eucalyptus trees and go out for daily training, under the watchful eyes of all kinds of lance-corporals and corporals. They attempt to knead us into shape using the iron discipline and regulations of the British military tradition. "Company D" is a real melting pot for young men who had arrived a few years earlier from various Jewish diasporas and who are trying to emulate the sabras. We run and crawl together; we eat from the same twisted mess-tins.

And on a more personal note: "it seems to me that our army years were highly meaningful to both of us, and that they significantly affected our adjustment into Israeli society."[18]

Haim Erez is another fellow recruit from "Company D." He is perhaps the only man from our shack in Training Base Four who went on to have an impressive military career. He ended up as commander of the IDF Armored Corps, in the rank of general. I've since learned that he, too, is a child survivor. Still, I wasn't sure whether we would have anything else in common. We met at Latrun, at the Armored Corps memorial site that he directs—a project that, since his retirement, has become his main occupation.

Haim has been the head of this project for years and was very proud to have directed the establishment of a military museum centered on Jewish soldiers during the Second World War, especially those who served in the Red Army. Our talk was quite friendly, but a far cry from the intimate, intellectual, and warm encounter with Guterman.

Haim Erez was once Heniek Rozenberg: a Jewish boy born in 1935 to a well-to-do family in Warsaw. His happy childhood ended on the first day of the Second World War. He distinctly recalls the bombardment of Warsaw in early September 1939: "I remember the noise, the fires, the run to the shelter." His father, like many Jewish men, fled eastward and reached Soviet-occupied

---

18 Yaakov Guterman, letter to author, April 2, 2015.

Bialystok. Only in December would Haim see his father again. The border was guarded by German and Soviet troops. "Mother decided to smuggle me alone and remain behind. I was four years old at the time. She tied a string around my neck with a piece of paper on which she wrote my father's name and address in Bialystok, and told me to look for him. She apparently bribed the Red Army guide to let me through. I walked in deep snow for hours and finally reached a village. A peasant woman took me in and brought me to my father next day." Haim's mother joined them later. His father decided for some reason to return to his family in German-occupied Warsaw, and Haim never saw him again.

Haim and his mother were deported by the Soviets from Bialystok to Siberia and later moved to Uzbekistan. His mother was arrested there and sentenced to ten years in a labor camp. Little Haim ended up in a Polish children's home and was transferred with General Anders's Polish Army to Tehran. He was one of the Jewish "Tehran Children," who arrived in Palestine in 1943. Following a short stay in the Atlit transit facility, he was brought to Nahalal in the Valley and was adopted by the Shniper family. As he recalled, "they were actually my new parents. They treated me like a son. They made a man out of me. They taught me to respect labor, agriculture, to love the country and its landscapes. It's this upbringing that shaped my decision to stay in the army and to care about the country."[19]

General Erez did not remember details or names from our military training in TB-4. I showed him old photos and archival documents. I wanted to stir his memory. The only names and faces he recognized were those of Yaakov Guterman, whom he had seen years later on TV, and our company commander, Lieutenant Moshe Shakuf. Haim, who lived in Nahalal, was brought from the recruiting station in nearby Afula to the army induction center in Tzrifin on August 24, 1950—the same day as myself. I wondered: how was it that General Haim Erez started his military career as a Grade-B soldier? As he explained,

> Nahalal was near the military airbase at Ramat David and I initially meant to train as a pilot. My temporary Grade-B health category prevented me from applying for flight training. That's how I ended up at Training Base Four. I have very good memories from there. We were a good bunch of people. The training was hard and serious. They busted our butts. It was Grade-B but there was strict discipline. We learned how to live with each other and how to be soldiers.[20]

---

19 "Against All Odds" (Israel: Israeli TV, Channel 1, 2013), film documentary; Haim Erez, interview by author, Latrun, May 2013.
20 Erez, interview.

Figure 4.1 IDF induction center in Tzrifin, August of 1954. From left to right: Dan Mador, the author, Dan Simonov.

Figure 4.2 At Training Base Four, from left to right: the author, Dan Mador, and Lieutenant Moshe Shakuf.

Figure 4.3 Author's squad in the sands of Nebi Rubin: Dan Mador, third from the left; Yaakov Guterman, ninth from the left; the author, fourth from the end of the row.

Figure 4.4 Commanding officer's parade at Training Base Four.

Figure 4.5 Commanding officer's parade: presenting arms.

Figure 4.6 Commanding officer's parade: at ease.

Figure 4.7 Lieutenant Colonel Dov Yirmiyahu inspecting company "D" during the commanding officer's parade.

Figure 4.8 Soldiers from Afula upon completion of basic training. Bottom row, *left to right*: the author, Moshe Gold, Amos Ben Arye, and Yair Hershkowitz. *Standing, from left to right*: Dan Mador, first from left; Dan Simonov, second; David Grinshpon, fifth.

Concluding Remarks

Learning about and meeting people who lived in Merhavia and Afula—as well as those who shared with me my military training at Training Base Four—has been a meaningful, educating, and emotional journey into the past. In these pages I've attempted to bring back to life the places I lived in during my first "Israeli" years. I've also tried to reexamine some aspects of my young self at that time.

At an early stage of my research on the nature of the kibbutz, I came across Reuven Shapira's study of kibbutz society, which dwells on the gap between the moral and humanistic ideology of the kibbutz and its everyday realities.[1] The kibbutz was supposedly guided by an ethos of egalitarianism; Shapira's book draws attention to the social stratification that existed in fact and to the presence there of a managerial elite. Since I bore a chip on my shoulder from my experience of Merhavia, his arguments at first seemed plausible to me. I could think of at least two privileged Merhavia "managers": Meir Yaari on top and Yaakov Shutzberg somewhere in the middle of the scale.[2] On deeper reflection, however, I decided that Shapira's approach was too simplistic and single minded. I'd also read an interesting and provocative article by the late British historian Tony Judt, in which he attempts to characterize the nature of the kibbutz based on his personal experiences.[3] Judt had spent some time in Israeli kibbutzim in the 1960s, when he was in his late teens. "These were provincial and rather conservative communities," says Judt, "their ideological rigidity camouflaging the limited horizon of many of their members." He also spoke of

---

1 Reuven Shapiro, *Transforming Kibbutz Research: Trust and Moral Leadership in the Rise and Decline of Democratic Cultures* (Cleveland, OH: New World Publishing, 2008).
2 Yaakov and Delka Shutzberg File, Merhavia Archive.
3 Tony Judt, "Kibbutz," accessed May 13, 2017, http://www.nybooks.com/daily/2010/01/18/kibbutz/.

"the extraordinary smugness of 'self-regard'" among them. I both agreed and disagreed with these remarks. There was, indeed, some ideological rigidity within the kibbutz movement, especially in its left wing. Judt's sweeping conclusions, however, don't do justice to the history of kibbutz society, to the significant differences between various kibbutzim, and to the heterogeneity of its membership. It also seems to me rather unjust to reach conclusions about the 'essence of the kibbutz' based on personal memories and impressions alone—a principle I've kept in mind in this book.

As to kibbutz Merhavia, in particular, and to my personal adjustment to it, I should admit that the Hashomer Hatzair mentality wasn't completely new to me when I first arrived. I had been a member of this youth movement in postwar Lodz and had absorbed some of its spirit there: the scouts' ethos, the unique bond between the councilors and the youth group members, and, not least, a somewhat vague but nevertheless powerful elitist notion—a conviction that we, the youth of Hashomer Hatzair, were better than those in other Zionist youth movements.[4] In the back of my mind at the time was also the fact that my aunts Pnina and Malcia, my mother's two younger sisters, had been members of Hashomer Hatzair in prewar Brzezany, and that Pnina was one of the founders of Merhavia. So I was not completely unprepared when I arrived at the kibbutz.

The notion I've had for years that Merhavia, besides sharing the general characteristics of kibbutz life, bore certain specific qualities stemming from the background and origin of its founders, was confirmed during the research for this book. A number of my Merhavia interviewees mentioned a "Galitzianer spirit" prevailing among the founding fathers of the kibbutz. It had both positive and negative aspects. One of the old-timers spoke of modesty, extreme earnestness, and restrained romanticism. Some of the younger generation, as well as people who joined Merhavia in later years, spoke in more critical tones. They mentioned the small-town mentality and the malicious gossip that affected relations among neighbors. The poet Tuvia Ruebner spoke of "the boring human landscape of Merhavia" that also held "those few extraordinary people."[5] At the same time, Merhavia was exceptional in the number of artists, musicians especially, who received their initial education in that kibbutz.

---

4 Shaul Paz, *Our Faces toward the Rising Sun: Members of the Pioneering Youth Movements in Israel: The Second Generation, 1947–1967* [in Hebrew] (Jerusalem: Bialik Institute and The Ben-Gurion Research Institute for the Study of Israel and Zionism, 2016), 33–34.

5 *Lea Goldberg to Tuvia Ruebner: Correspondence* [in Hebrew] (Tel Aviv: Sifriat Hapoalim Publishing House, 2017), 158.

Concluding Remarks

The filmmaker Michal Bat Adam, who lived in Merhavia throughout her adolescence, summed up this duality succinctly: "On the one hand there was open-mindedness in matters of spirit; and on the other interpersonal relations reminded me of soil that's been tamped down and never been aired." Harsh and highly judgmental attitudes were expressed at times during the general assembly meetings. Some kibbutz members were attacked openly and personally. Tuvia Yaari, Meir Yaari's younger brother, excelled in such accusations. Meir Yaari, himself, wasn't an easy person to deal with, both inside and outside the kibbutz. Yet by contrast, there were figures such as Zvi Vardi and the Mintzer brothers, who displayed an exceptional humaneness. Nor was kibbutz society entirely insular: some members, like the Ruebners and the Herutis, maintained close and meaningful contacts with their professional and spiritual friends in the cities.

What was my own acculturation to kibbutz life like? What were the strong and the weak points in my absorption by kibbutz society and my adaptation to it, mostly within my peer group, Gefen? I did succeed at school. I dressed and looked like the others. Yet when it came to hard physical labor, held high in the scale of values in the kibbutz, I barely even tried. I did not excel in sports. That said, I did not lag behind in the hikes and marches across the country, a significant element in any youngster's "Israelization."[6] I always joined happily in the sing-alongs, an activity which served as a sort of catharsis for the group.[7]

As to the process of socialization of young immigrants and Holocaust survivors within the kibbutzim in the late 1940s and the 1950s: Oz Almog rightfully remarks that "the anti-Diaspora ethos and the negativity toward its associated stereotypes, produced paternalism, arrogance and sometimes even rejection."[8] My case wasn't extreme, but the Diaspora-type nicknaming stuck to me and stings me to this day. Then, of course, there was the complex issue of growing up physically and sexually. I was rather short, and physically unlike the "leaders" in the group who already had their first girlfriends. What finally drove me out of Merhavia was what Almog refers to as anti-intellectualism and negative attitudes toward higher education.[9]

---

6 Oz Almog, *The Sabra: The Creation of the New Jew* (Berkeley: University of California Press, 2000), 174–81.
7 Almog, *The Sabra*, 235–39; Paz, *Our Faces*, 336–44.
8 Almog, *The Sabra*, 88.
9 Ibid., 143–46.

The move from kibbutz Merhavia to Afula was a regression of sorts. From a highly valued pioneering society, I switched into a much less prestigious small-town life. Yet in many ways, I was more comfortable. It seemed more like my previous life in postwar Lodz. I felt less inferior than with my peer group in Merhavia, though of course I never became part of the Afula's sabra elite. I notice that when speaking to my Afula interviewees, what seems to have interested me most was the way in which friendships and couples formed among the adolescents: for all that passed me by. My only real friend in Afula was Nelu, a newcomer, like myself. I envied Dudu, another newcomer, who was very successful with the girls. Some of the interviewees admitted that the absorption of immigrant students was a painful business and regretted their attitudes toward the newcomers in their later lives.

Most of the Afula-born interviewees and those who settled there as children had fond memories of that town. My own memories of Afula are mixed. When I look back upon my army service, there is not much to be proud of. Although I managed to complete my tough basic training at Training Base Four without a major disaster, during the rest of my military service, all I did was paperwork.

Comparing my first years in Israel with my postwar and post-Holocaust years in Lodz, it seems, perhaps surprisingly, that I was happier in Lodz than in Israel. My relative standing among my peers was much higher in Lodz than in either Merhavia or Afula. In Lodz, I was the teacher's pet; in Israel, I was just one of the bunch, if that. Only years later, when I started my academic studies and career, would my self-esteem recover itself. That's when I began to see myself as part of an intellectual milieu. Still, the beginnings were apparent already in my Afula high-school years. I continued to devour books, as I had done previously in Brzezany and in Lodz. Although my Polish fell into disuse, my Hebrew improved and became my principal tongue. My knowledge of English steadily improved. Already during my senior years in the Afula high school I'd read some of the English language paperbacks popular at the time, including James Jones's *From Here To Eternity*, Norman Mailer's *The Naked and the Dead*, and Irwin Shaw's *The Young Lions*. During my years at Hebrew University and at Harvard, I studied Russian. When Eastern Europe opened up in the late 1980s and early 1990s, I started traveling to Poland, Russia, and Ukraine. I regained my Polish and improved my Russian and Ukrainian. In recent years I've also immersed myself in Yiddish. Although my principal identity is Jewish and Israeli, I feel at home, culturally at least, in New York, London, Warsaw, Moscow, Kiev, and Lviv.

Concluding Remarks

The era in Israel of which I am writing has passed. I hope that this book succeeds in presenting some features of society in the early years of the State, and that it bears witness to the adjustment of one young immigrant—one among thousands—to the realities of a new life in Israel.

Bibliography

Almog, Oz. *Farewell to 'Srulik': Changing Values among the Israeli Elite* [in Hebrew]. Haifa and Or Yehuda: Haifa University Publishers and Zmora-Bitan Publishers, 2004.

———. *The Sabra: The Creation of the New Jew*. Berkeley: University of California Press, 2000.

Bat Adam, Michal. *An Imagined Autobiography* [in Hebrew]. Tel Aviv: Yediot Aharonot Publishers, 2002.

Ben-Arie, Amos. *The Ben-Arie Family Stories* [in Hebrew]. Tel Aviv: Tirosh Publishing House, 2013.

Ben Dov, Nitza. *War Lives: On the Army, Revenge, Grief, and the Consciousness of War in Israeli Fiction* [in Hebrew]. Jerusalem: Shocken Publishing House, 2016.

Bettelheim, Bruno. *The Children of the Dream*. London: The Macmillan Company, 1969.

Cnaani, David, ed. *Sefer Merhavia, Kibbutz Hashomer Hatzair* [in Hebrew]. Merhavia: Sifriat Hapoalim Publishers, 1961.

The City of Jezreel—Afula, 1925–1950 [in Hebrew]. Afula: Afula Local Council, 1950.

Elon, Amos. *The Israelis: Founders and Sons*. New York: Bantam Books, 1972.

Evens, T. M. S. *Two Kinds of Rationality: Kibbutz Democracy and Generational Conflict*. Minneapolis: University of Minnesota Press, 1995.

Evens, Terrence M. S. "Stigma and Morality in a Kibbutz." In *A Composite Portrait of Israel*, edited by Emmanuel Marx, chapter 8. New York: Academic Press, 1980.

Frankel, Alona. *Teen Years* [in Hebrew]. Tel Aviv: Am Oved Publishers, 2009.

Giladi, Dan. "Afula: The Valley Town or a Town Facing the Valley." In *Jezreel Valley, 1900–1967* [in Hebrew], edited by Mordechai Naor. Jerusalem: Ben Zvi Institute Publishers, 1993.

Gispan-Grinberg, Tamar. "Mural Art in the Communal Dining Halls of the Kibbutz Haartzi in the Years 1950–1967." *Cathedra* 135 (2010): 151–79.

Gitai, Rivka, ed. *Efratia Gitai: Correspondence, 1929–1994* [in Hebrew]. Tel Aviv: Miskal Publishers, 2011.

Guterman, Simcha. *Leaves out of the Fire* [in Hebrew]. Jerusalem and Tel Aviv: Yad Vashem and Moreshet Publishers, 2004.

Guttman, Nava. *Processes of Coping and Adaptation in Stress* [in Hebrew]. Master's thesis, Bar-Ilan University, 1989.

Hacohen, Dvora. *Immigrants in Turmoil: Mass Immigration and Its Absorption in Israel, 1948–1953* [in Hebrew]. Jerusalem: Ben Zvi Institute Publishers, 1994.

Bibliography

Halamish, Aviva. *Meir Yaari—A Collective Biography: The First Fifty Years, 1897–1947* [in Hebrew]. Tel Aviv: Am Oved Publishers, 2009.

———. *Meir Yaari—The Rebbe from Merhavia: The State Years* [in Hebrew]. Tel Aviv: Am Oved Publishers, 2013.

Holzman, Avner. "Jezreel Valley in Hebrew Literature." In *Jezreel Valley, 1900–1967* [in Hebrew], edited by Mordechai Naor, 215–27. Jerusalem: Ben Zvi Institute Publishers, 1993.

Inbari, Assaf. *Home* [in Hebrew]. Tel Aviv: Yedioth Aharonoth Publishers, 2009.

Judt, Tony. "Kibbutz." Accessed May 13, 2017. http://www.nybooks.com/daily/2010/01/18/kibbutz.

Kahana, Freddy. *Neither Town Nor Village: The Architecture of the Kibbutz, 1910–1990* [in Hebrew]. Ramat Gan: Yad Tabenkin, 2011.

Kenaz, Yehoshua. *Heart Murmur* [in Hebrew]. Tel Aviv: Am Oved Publishers, 1986.

———. *Infiltration*. South Royalton, VT: Zoland Books, 2003.

Kishon, Ephraim. *Partachia, My Love* [in Hebrew]. Tel Aviv: Sifriat Maariv Publishers, 1976.

Kochavi, Daviv (Starec). *Tears among the Waves: From Exodus to Jerusalem*. New York: Epoch Publishing, 2008.

Lapid, Yair. *Memories after My Death* [in Hebrew]. Jerusalem: Keter Books, 2010.

Lieblich, Amia. *Kibbutz Makom: Report from an Israeli Kibbutz*. New York: Pantheon Books, 1981.

Lissak, Moshe, ed. *The History of the Jewish Community in Eretz-Israel since 1882: Israel—The First Decade* [in Hebrew]. Jerusalem: The Israel Academy for Sciences and Humanities and The Bialik Institute, 2009.

Marx, Emmanuel, ed. *A Composite Portrait of Israel*. New York: Academic Press, 1980.

Naor, Mordechai, "Jezreel Valley—The Cradle of the Kibbutzim." In *Jezreel Valley, 1900–1967* [in Hebrew], edited by Mordechai Naor, 54–71. Jerusalem: Ben Zvi Institute Publishers, 1993.

Naor, Mordechai, ed. *Jezreel Valley, 1900–1967* [in Hebrew]. Jerusalem: Ben Zvi Institute Publishers, 1993.

Near, Henry. *The Kibbutz Movement: A History*. Vol. 2, *Crisis and Achievement, 1939–1995*. Oxford: The Littman Library of Jewish Civilization, 2007.

Neeman, Yael. *We Were the Future* [in Hebrew]. Tel Aviv: Achuzat Bayit Publishers, 2011.

Paz, Sasha. *Il Monsignore* [in Hebrew]. Jerusalem: Carmel Publishers, 2006.

Peri, Yoram. *Between Battles and Ballots: Israeli Military in Politics*. Cambridge: Cambridge University Press, 1983.

Perlmutter, Amos. *Military and Politics in Israel: Nation-Building and Role Expansion*. London: Frank Cass, 1969.

Ruebner, Tuvia. *And Hastens to His Place, 1953–1989* [in Hebrew]. Tel Aviv: Sifriat Hapoalim Publishers, 1990.

———. *Ein Langes Kurzes Leben* [in Hebrew]. Tel Aviv: Keshev Publishing House, 2006.

———. *Gam zot ra'u eynay* [in Hebrew]. Tel Aviv: Keshev Publishing House, 2007.

———. *Last: 2011–2012* [in Hebrew]. Tel Aviv: Keshev Publishing House, 2013.

Segev, Tom. *1949—The First Israelis* [in Hebrew]. Jerusalem: Domino Publishers, 1984.

Sela, Maya. "Interview with Amos Gitai." *Haaretz*, April 14, 2011.

Shabtai, Aharon. *Kibbutz: Poems* [in Hebrew]. Tel Aviv: Hakibbutz Hameuchad Publishers, 1973.
Shabtai, Edna. *For Love Is Strong as Death* [in Hebrew]. Jerusalem: Keter Publishers, 1986.
———. "Since Their Son Disappeared." *Yediot Aharonot*, October 16, 1987.
Shahar, Natan, et al., eds. *Songs and Poems from the Israeli Valley* [in Hebrew]. Bnei Brak: Hakibbutz Hameuchad Publishers, 2005.
Shapira, Anita. "The Kibbutz and the State." *The Jewish Review of Books* 2 (Summer 2010), 5–6.
Shapiro, Reuven. *Transforming Kibbutz Research: Trust and Moral Leadership in the Rise and Decline of Democratic Cultures*. Cleveland, OH: New World Publishing, 2008.
Shehory-Rubin, Z., "Dr. Hanka Weinberg-Herouti: The Pediatrician from Merhavia—The First Woman Doctor 'Kibbutznik' in the Kibbutz Ha'artzi." *Harefuah: Journal of the Israel Medical Association* 154, no. 7 (July 2015): 460–63.
Shepher, Israel, and Reuven Shapiro. *Kibbutz: Continuity and Change* [in Hebrew]. Tel Aviv: The Open University of Israel, Unit 8–9, 1998.
Spiro, Melford E. and Audrey G. *Children of the Kibbutz*. Cambridge, MA: Harvard University Press, 1975.
Tallmon (Tillman), Shlomo. *The Way It Was: Merhavia, 1931–1989* [in Hebrew]. Tel Aviv: Self-published, 1990.
Taubman, Orit. *Hardiness, Mental Health, and Coping Processes during Basic Military Training* [in Hebrew]. Master's thesis, Bar-Ilan University, 1993.
Tsameret, Zvi, and Hanna Yablonka, eds. *The First Decade, 1948–1958* [in Hebrew]. Jerusalem: Ben Zvi Institute Publishers, 1997.
Turgan, Sagi. *Battle Leadership: The Commander Image in the IDF and Its Origin, 1936–1956* [in Hebrew]. Master's thesis, Hebrew University, 2001.
———. *Training Combat: Leadership in the IDF, 1949–1956* [in Hebrew]. PhD diss., Hebrew University, 2008.
Tzahor, Zeev. *We Were the Revival* [in Hebrew]. Tel Aviv: Hakibbutz Hameuchad Publishers, 2015.
Vardi, Zvi. *Orhot Hevra* [in Hebrew]. Merhavia: Sifriat Hapoalim Publishers, 1946.
Vilnai, Zeev. *Afula: Jezreel Town* [in Hebrew]. Afula: Afula Local Council, 1966.
Weintraub-Klein, Ruta. *Other Days* [in Hebrew]. Kibbutz Dalia: Maarechet Publishing House, 2002.
Yablonka, Hanna. "Immigrants from Europe and Holocaust Consciousness." In *The First Decade, 1948-1958* [in Hebrew], edited by Zvi Tsameret and Hanna Yablonka. Jerusalem: Ben Zvi Insitute Publishers, 1997.
Yeshurun, Helit. *How Did You Do It? Interviews with Poets* [in Hebrew]. Tel Aviv: Hakibbutz Hameuchad Publishers, 2016.
Zeira, Yaara. "Expanses of Tel Aviv and the Confines of Merhavia." *Bemakhane Hanachal*, November 28, 1984.

Index

Note: Page numbers followed by 'n' denotes notes

A
Abigail 27, 56, 64
acculturation, 19, 114
adolescents, 4, 14, 27, 34, 51, 56, 80, 81, 115
Afikim, 9, 10
Afula, 1, 5, 7, 19, 43, 46, 52-53, 66–95, 111
    housing and population, 68
    independence day in, 93
    school system in, 70
Afula High School, 2, 73, 80, 115
Agnon, Shmuel Yosef, 66
Al Hamishmar, 29, 49, 55
Aliyat Hanoar, 5, 7
Almog, Oz, ix, 114
Aluma, Shlomit, 25
Amir, Eli, 67
Arab Legion, 76, 79
Austria, 2, 10, 39, 87
Averbukhs, 77
Avni, Yehezkel, 29n27
Avraham (Buma) Yassour, 20

B
Bahevra newsletter, 18n1, 20n5
Banska Bistrica, 43
Bar-Adon, Pessah, 40
Bat Adam, Michal, 52, 53, 54n88, 55n92, 114
Beit Alfa, 11, 16, 51, 66, 73
Beit Hashita, 66, 82, 83
Beit Zvi, 23, 51
Bela, 26, 27, 63, 64
Ben Dov, Nitza, 99n8
Ben-Gurion, David, 8, 31, 32, 101
Ben-Gurion University, 13, 74, 81
Ben Shemen boarding school, 10
Berkowitz, Yitzhak Dov, 66

Betar Zionist movement, 72
Bettelheim, Bruno, 14
Beyt Sefer Yami, 3
Bleiberg-Hardof, Nira, 2, 89
Bodo, Yaakov, 71, 88
Boy Takes Girl (film), 53, 54n89
Brandstetter, Shimon, 41
Brzezany, viii, 4, 41, 113, 115

C
childhood, vii, viii, 11, 25, 44, 51, 58, 59, 77, 78, 81, 84, 87, 88, 98, 105
Christianity, 81
class conflict, 32
Cnaani, David, 18n2, 19, 21n7, 24n15
Cohen, Amiram, 40n56
Cohen-Yarom, Yael, 83, 83n36, 84–86
communism, 81, 85
Company "D," 100, 103, 105, 106, 111

D
Dagan, Arie, 28
Damari, Shoshana, 2
Davar Layeladim, 90
Dayan, Moshe, 97, 101
Dayan, Shmuel, 66
diaspora, 7, 26, 69, 106, 114

E
Economy Committee, Haifa
economic crisis, 68, 75
egalitarianism, 7, 10, 112
Ehud, 57, 64, 65
Electric Corporation, 84, 85, 86, 90
Elon, Amos, 7n19
Eretz Israel, 5, 18, 39

Erez, Haim, 106, 107
Evens, Terrence M. S., ix, 35n39
Exodus, 72, 73
Eyn Harod, 22, 44, 66, 105

F
fascism, 39
Feibish, Dudu, 86, 87, 88n44, 89, 90, 91
First World War, 2, 16, 18, 70, 83, 87
Fishl, 4
Fleisher, Ada, 31
Fleisher, Kuba, 32
Forverts (Yiddish newspaper), 74
Frankel, Alona, 3
From Here To Eternity (Jones), 115

G
Galatz, Romania, 81
Galila (ship), 1–3, 6, 15, 105
Galicia, viii, 18, 21, 24, 42, 52, 54, 57, 89
Galitzianer, 47, 113
Gamzou, Haim, 40
Gan Shmuel, 49, 59
Garden Suburb concept, 9
gar'inim, 17
Gdud Haavoda, 86
Gefen group, 23, 26, 28, 31, 53, 55, 56, 57, 58, 60, 64, 114
Geller, Janek, 1
General assembly meetings, 31, 35, 39, 39n54, 40n55, 114
Geva, 34
Giladi, Dan, 68n4
Giladi, Ethan, 48, 49
Gispan-Grinberg, Tamar, 9n25
Gitai, Rivka, 41n58
Gitai-Margalit, Efratia, 36, 37, 37n46, 38, 39, 39n50, 40
Gitai-Weinraub, Munio, 40, 41
Giv'at Hamoreh, 3, 25
golah-type Jews, 7
Golan-Ben Yaakov, Yona, 37n45
Goldberg, Leah, 45, 51
Goldblat, Jetka, 34n38, 41, 42n61
Goren, Avraham, 27, 28
grade B soldiers, 96, 97, 99, 102, 106, 107
Grol, Lusiek, 30, 31, 33, 42n63, 43
Guterman, Yaakov, 104, 105, 106n18, 107, 109
Guterman, Simcha, 105
Guttman, Nava, 102n11

H
Haaretz, 3, 4n5

Hacohen, Dvora, 6n9, 7n16
Ha'emek, 66
Hahotrim group, 46
Haifa, 1, 3, 5, 6, 16, 23, 26, 41, 52, 55, 58, 60, 61, 71, 73, 75, 79, 105
Haifa City Museum, 3n2
Haifa port, 3, 5, 6, 71, 73, 81
hakhatser hagdola, 31
hakhshara, 19
Hakibbutz Haartzi movement, 13, 16, 21, 37, 57
Hakibbutz Hameuchad Movement 13n36, 50n80, 50n81, 62, 67n3
Halamish, Aviva, 22, 23n11, 28n25
Haleli, Y., 19n4
Halevi-Etzioni, Hava, 80n29
Handelsman, David *see* Cnaani, David
Hanegbi, David, 47
Hanoar Haoved, 84
Hardof-Bleiberg, Nira, 89n47, 90, 91, 95
Harpaz, Barke, 51, 52
Harpaz-Reich, Naomi, 51, 52
hashlama eretz-israelit, 17, 20
hashlamot, 17
Hashomer Hatzair youth movement, 10, 12, 17, 27, 36, 39, 43, 47, 113
Hebrew Tarbut high school, 86
Hershkowitz, Maya, 82, 83
Hershkowitz, Yair, 82, 95, 111
Heruti, Yitzhak, 30, 35, 36, 37, 38, 38n48, 40, 41
Herzig, Moshe, 74
Herzliyah High School, 37, 39, 40
heterogeneous community, 47
heterosexual activity, 13
Hillel, Ayin, 67
Hirszfeld, Ariel, 67
Hoffman, Ferenc, 3
Holocaust, 1, 29, 45, 58, 71, 72, 75, 81, 84
Holocaust survivors, 2, 3, 10, 13, 21, 42, 52, 72, 114
Holocaust Day ceremony, 60
Holzman, Avner, 67n2
Home (Inbari), 9
Horowitz, Hava, 79–80
Hudson River, 2
humane personality, 24

I
immigrants, vii, 2, 3, 5–8, 12, 17, 26, 30, 32, 35, 48, 67, 71, 73, 74, 82, 88, 96
Inbari, Assaf, 9, 10n26
Infiltration (novel), ix, 97, 98

Israeli Defense Forces (IDF), vii–ix, 79, 96, 100, 101, 102
Israeli legation, Warsaw, 2

J
Jewish Agency, 2
Jewish community, 7, 38, 72, 105
Jewish immigrants, 2
Jewish moshavim, 66
Jezreel Valley, vii, 1, 16, 66, 67, 97
Jones, James, 115
Jordan Valley, 9
Judt, Tony, 112

K
Kagan, Eliezer, 74, 78, 90
Kahana, Freddy, 9n24
Kahan, Dorothy, 40
Kamionka, 4
Kaufman, Richard, 67
Kehilat Zion, 67
Kenaz, Yehoshua, ix, 97–99
Kfar Yehezkel, 75
Kfar Yeladim, 69, 70, 76
khadar haokhel, 9, 30
khatser, 19
Khavatzelet group, 21
khevrat yeladim, 20
khevrot noar, 17
kibbutzniks, 7
"Kibbutz" (poem), 49, 50
Kiryat Haim, 73
Kishon, Ephraim, 3
Klein, Zvi, 42, 46, 47
Kochavi, Arik, 71
Kochavi, David, 72n11, 73, 74, 91
kolektiviut raayonit, 31
Kolron Cinema, 69
komuna, 44
kooperatzia, 16
Kremlin, 16
Kritz, Reuven, 67
kvutza, 11, 12, 27, 28, 29

L
Lapid, Yair, 79n28
Lapid, Yosef "Tomi," 78–80
Lissak, Moshe, 6n8
Lodz, viii, 1-5, 26, 36, 56, 113, 115
Lurie, Shalom, 20, 46, 48
Lurie, Zvi, 36

M
maabarot, 6, 7
Mador, Dan, 85, 95, 108, 109, 111
Mador-Mendershausen, Alfred-Abraham, 85, 87
Mailer, Norman, 115
Malcia, 5, 113
Mapai, 31, 58, 77, 84
Mapam, 31, 34, 58, 60
Megilat Hameah (Rachel), 18
Meirson, Golda, 16
Memories after My Death (Lapid), 78
Merhavia, 1, 3–5, 13, 16–65, 68, 90, 113
    educational system in, 20, 21
    gar'inim, 17
    hashlamot, 17, 18
    kibbutz Haartzi movement, 16, 21, 28, 57
    social dilemma in, 18
metapelet, 9
Mikve Israel agricultural school, 42
Mintzer, Yoel, ix, 30, 35n40, 41n59, 55, 56n93, 64
Mintzer, Husia, 32, 34, 39
Mintzer-Heruti, Ruthi, ix, 56
Mishmar Haemek, 16, 20, 22, 24, 33, 37, 56, 66, 67
Mishmar Layeladim, 90
moetset hatnuah, 32
Moshe Man, 33
Mount Gilboa, 25

N
Nahalal, 66, 67, 97, 107
The Naked and the Dead (Mailer), 115
Naor, Mordehai, 66n1
Narkis group, 11
Nassau, Erich, Prof., 39, 40, 40n57, 69, 70
Naveh, Menahem, 27, 28n23
Near, Henry, 8n21
Nebi Rubin, 103, 104, 109
Neeman, Yael, 10, 11
Nelu, 71, 84, 86, 94, 95, 115
Neta group, 17
Nicknames, nicknaming, 12, 28, 54, 71, 114
Nir, Reuven, ix
Nir, Yitzhak, ix

O
Or, Emda, 74–77
Or-Averbukh, Theodore, 76, 77n23, 78, 82

Or-Averbukh, Yosef, 76, 77
Ora, 5, 87, 88, 89, 90, 95

P
Pagis, Dan, 45
Palestine, 1, 4, 5, 7, 9–11, 16, 17, 20, 21, 36, 37–39, 42, 43, 46, 52, 69, 70, 72–74
Paz, Sasha, 77, 81, 81n32, 82, 83
Paz, Shaul, 113
peer group, vii, 11–14, 27, 28, 34, 53, 57, 115
Pepka, 5
Peri, Eliezer, 34
Perlmutter, Amos, 101n10
Perlstein, Khava, 103
personality cult, 23
Planty group, 17, 18, 19
Pnina, 1, 4–5, 26
pochkes, 44
Poland, viii, 2, 6, 17–20, 26, 31, 40–42, 59, 60, 74, 76
Polish Jews, 74
Porat, Orna, 40
Poveglia, 2
project method, 12
Proter-Porat, Yosef, 40

R
Ramat Gan, 1
Ramat Hakovesh, 13
Ramat Yohanan, 14
Rand, Itsio, 57
Rapoport, Natan, 52
Reich, Eliezer, 28
Reich, Khancia, 58, 59
Riftin, Kuba, 33
Righteous Gentiles medal, 60
Rimon group, 21
Rothem, Yaakov, 41
Rubin, Adam, 52, 53
Ruebner, Galila, 44n66
Ruebner, Tuvia, 43, 44n64, 45n68, 51, 53, 113

S
Sabra, Sabras, vii, 13, 17, 26, 57, 82, 85, 86, 97, 99, 100, 106
Sarafand, 96
Scapegoat, 67
Schulz, Bruno, 42
Schumacher, Israel, 37
Second World War, 2, 17, 21, 52, 83, 86, 97, 106

semel bogrim, 27
Sha'ar Ha'aliya transit camp, 5, 6
Shabtai, Aharon, 49, 50, 50n80, 51
Shabtai, Edna, 47, 48, 48n76, 51, 52
Shabtai, Yaakov, 47, 48, 49
Shahar, Ehud, 27, 57, 65, 101
Shahar, Nathan, 67n3
Shakuf, Moshe, 103, 107
Shalhevet group, 21, 52
Shapira, Anita, 8n22
Shapira, Reuven, 8n23, 112
Shatzman, Poldi, 100
Shaw, Irwin, 115
Shaya, 5, 26, 61
Shehory-Rubin, Z., 39n52
Shepher, Israel, 8n23
Shibolet group, 53
shikun vatikim, 31
Shkhunat Hapoalim, 68, 70, 77, 83, 84, 88, 92
Shlonsky, Avraham, 45
Shutzberg, Yaakov (Janek), 29, 29n28, 30, 32, 33, 42, 47, 56, 112
Sinai-Simonov, Dan, 83, 85, 86, 95, 108
Sinai-Edelstein, Naomi, 83, 85n39
Six Day War, 48
social activities, 20, 21
social cohesiveness, 20
Socialist-Zionist ideology, 18
Spiro, Audrey G., 12
Spiro, Melford E., 12
Spiros, 11
St. Luke's, 6
Stigma and Morality, 34
Strauss, Ludwig, 45
Syrian Arabs, 75

T
Tallmon, Shlomo, 21n6
Talmi, Avraham (Bozhik), 28
Tel Aviv, x, 1, 4, 17, 20, 22, 23, 33, 36, 37, 43, 47, 48, 51, 67, 85, 87, 90
Tenenbaum, Binyamin, 52
teudat bagrut, 10
Tharlev, Yoram, 67
Tikhon Hadash high school, 48, 51
Training Base Four (TB-4), 96–111
Tsamri, Esther, ix, 31, 57, 58, 59, 59n99, 60, 61, 63, 64
Tsamri, Ezra, ix, 30, 31, 57, 58, 64
Tsamri, Yaakov, 39, 49

Turgan, Sagi, 97n3
Tzahor, Zeev, 13
Tzrifin, 96, 103, 107

U
Umanski, Dani, 49
Unzere Kinder, 1
US Air Force, 72

V
Valley Hospital, 39, 40, 68–70, 78, 79, 83–89
Vardi, Shlomit, 25, 27n22, 32, 33
Vardi, Zvi, 23, 24, 25, 36, 40, 114
verbal aggression, 12
Vilnai, Zeev, 69n8

W
War of Independence, 10, 46, 50, 59, 69, 71, 76–77, 82, 84-86
Weinberg-Heruti, Hanka, 36, 37, 37n47, 38, 40, 41
Weintraub-Klein, Ruta, 42, 42n62
Weintraub, Ryszard, 31, 33, 42, 46, 63
Weiss, Gideon, 26, 60, 61n100
We Were the Future (Neeman), 10

Y
Yaari, Meir, 16, 17, 19, 21, 22, 24, 28, 32, 33, 58, 61
Yaari, Tuvia, 22, 32, 39, 47, 61, 112, 114
Yablonka, Hanna, 7n15
Yakhimovitch, Sheli, 29
yaldat khutz, 54
yaldei gola, 21, 26
yaldei khutz, 12, 20–21, 26, 28, 58
Yarkoni, Yaffa, 2
Yassour, Avraham (Buma), 20, 32, 33
Yehiam, 10, 11
Yemenite woman, 38
Yeshurun, Helit, 50n81
Yirmiyah, Dov, 97, 111
Yishuv, 7, 66
Yonatan, Natan, 67
The Young Lions (Shaw), 115

Z
Zamir, David, 34, 35
Zamir, Uzi, 34, 35
Zamir group, 53
Zeev, 1, 5, 68, 70, 77, 84, 90
Zeira, Yaara, 49n79
ZIM shipping company, 2

www.ingramcontent.com/pod-product-compliance
Lightning Source LLC
Chambersburg PA
CBHW071822230426
43670CB00013B/2542